Andrew Day, Martin Dunford,
Jonathan Knight, James War

740007192049

The publishers assert their right to use *Cool Camping*
as a trademark of Punk Publishing Ltd.

Cool Camping: Kids (3rd edition)

This edition published in the UK in 2017 by

Punk Publishing Ltd.
81 Rivington Street, London EC2A 3AY
www.punkpublishing.co.uk
www.coolcamping.com
Copyright © Punk Publishing Ltd 2017

A catalogue record of this book is available from the British Library.

ISBN 978-1-906889-67-8

10 8 6 4 2 1 3 5 7 9

contents

introduction

Parents. We know you love holidays. But chances are that since the kids arrived the very concept of holidays has been redefined. Tears, tantrums and tiredness can mean an exhausting experience for all, leaving you in need of – well, another holiday.

Luckily, camping and children go together like marshmallows and hot chocolate. The idea of racing around in the outdoors, building dens, making friends, getting muddy and sleeping under the stars is, quite frankly, far more agreeable than a week at a hotel or at your Aunt Mary's. And as your kids busy themselves with worms and frisbees and fairies, not only does it take the pressure off you, but witnessing them have so much fun is actually one of the great, underrated pleasures of being a parent.

Picking a campsite that will keep you and your children happy, however, is not always as straightforward as it might seem; children, rather like adults, bring with them a long list of their own specific demands. It is with this in mind that we have compiled this third edition of *Cool Camping: Kids*, designed and written specifically for you and the children in your life. We have steered clear of the big corporate sites with chicken-in-a-basket and fruit machines in the clubhouse, wave machines in the swimming pool and karaoke until dawn. Your children would probably have loved that, but we have a hunch that you might not.

Instead we have picked a stellar cast of some of the most family-friendly sites on offer in the country, all of which exemplify the free-spirited sense of adventure that *Cool Camping* is all about.

This latest edition has more sites than ever, now featuring a whopping total of 80 fantastic family campsites, every one of which has been vetted and selected by us and, wherever possible, by our kids. We think that you and your children, whatever their age, are going to love the sites covered in these pages, too.

We want you to have the most fun possible with your kids, wherever you are camping so, as always, we have included, alongside our reviews, a thorough information section for each site detailing all the practical aspects of your holiday. This includes extensive info about onsite and offsite fun, with listings for local attractions that children are bound to enjoy. And, in the name of serious research, we've even tested the best places for local homemade ice cream, the tastiest fish and chips and the best family-friendly pubs to add to the Food and Drink sections.

Part of the pleasure of camping with children is dispensing with the domestic clutter of everyday life. Without sounding too Zen about it, there's a purity to camping that's hard to replicate in 'normal' life, giving you time to completely connect with your children, rather than having to

worry about what you are going to put into their lunchboxes, if they've learned enough for their spelling tests and whether or not they've got nits.

The focus of 'all-in-this-together' fun is food and mealtimes, so we've included a cooking section (p126) with some yummy treats you can easily put together on a barbecue or campfire, and which your children will love to help out with, too.

There's also a games section (p82), so you can make your own fun on site, and we've picked a selection of our favourite festivals (p222) that are just as enjoyable for kids as they are for parents. Finally, we've assembled a list of the best family-friendly campervan hire companies in the country (p174), so even if your car is too small to fit all the camping clobber inside, you can find a new set of well designed wheels that will get you on the road.

And because we've chosen sites over a wide geographical area, whichever part of the country you are in we're pretty sure you'll find some place in *Cool Camping: Kids* that you and your children will love.

A few final words to those undecided readers who haven't tried camping before – just give it a go! The worst that could happen is a weekend of wet weather and a wasted few quid. But on the other hand, it might just be your best-ever holiday together – and the start of a wonderful, new family adventure in the great outdoors…

Happiest camping!

campsite locator

campsites at a glance

a parent's guide

Kids just love camping. There are few phrases that elicit more delight than 'let's go camping!' 'Want some chocolate?' might come a close second!

the best fun

You'd be hard pressed to find a child that doesn't jump at the chance to forgo baths, cook on campfires and spend the night sleeping in a field. Whether you are entertaining your own children or some you've borrowed for the weekend, camping is some of the best fun that children and grown-ups can have together – out in the fresh air, without all the trappings of modern life and taking a break from the daily routine. And the great thing is that it doesn't really need all that much planning in advance, doesn't have to cost very much and pretty much anyone can do it, regardless of where they live or whether or not they drive a car.

reconnecting with kids

Breaking out of the normal routine of everyday life is also a brilliant way to reconnect with your children and spend some quality time together away from the usual distractions and necessities of life at home. And children really love the fact that, for a few days, you can all kick back and dispense with those phrases that drive us all mad: 'If you don't put your shoes on now we're going to miss the bus/Where's your book bag?/You didn't forget your lunch box again did you?/Is that the time? We're going to be late that govern most parents' and kids' lives. Camping and children are a match made in heaven – just keep a few basic rules in mind and you'll have some very, very happy, fun-sized campers on your hands indeed.

cutting the clutter

We don't want to start *Cool Camping: Kids* with a long list of complicated items for you to rush out and buy. Camping isn't about a retail experience: it's about a real experience. Of course, if you want to go to a camping shop and spend a hefty sum on lots of plasticky nylon bits of camping equipment then go ahead; there's no doubt such retail therapy can be a lot of fun. Just remember that it's not strictly necessary and it's certainly not essential. Camping is all about cutting a lot of clutter out of life. So break free from the screen addiction that dominates life and leave the plastic at home. Certainly, you can, if you are very well organised, equip each child with a torch, a disposable camera and a backpack full of favourite toys and books, but it might be much more sensible to reckon on the fact that they'll probably lose all those things the moment they get out of the car.

getting your tent legs

A happy camping trip should be framed by the experience of getting out into a beautiful part of the country, perhaps somewhere you've never visited before, throwing up a tent (perhaps a borrowed one), and then getting down to some serious fun with your kids. It's as simple as that: homemade fun, like homemade food, is our favourite variety. As well as saving money, cutting back on kit will make your trip a lot less stressful. Squeezing everything you own, plus the kitchen

sink, into your car is probably not that much fun for you, or for your family. There are a few basic things to bring, or to do, when you are planning a camping trip with children. If you're first-time campers, then it's probably best to borrow kit and head out for a night or two, not all that far from home. This way you can work out exactly what you need to take for a longer trip further afield. Don't start your inaugural trip with a 10-hour drive to some far-flung spot, because camping close to home is best until you really get your tent legs: long car trips are tiring and, wherever you live, there are sure to be some tip-top campsites nearby.

choosing a site

When it comes to site selection, remember that pre-warned is pre-armed. Find out what facilities are available beforehand. We all have different tastes, and so do our children, and while some kids will love the lack of boundaries of the more basic sites, others will respond very positively to play

facilities and spanking-clean showers being laid on. Try to arrive at your site in plenty of time before dark, so that your kids have time to orientate themselves, explore new surroundings and perhaps even make a new friend or two. Pitching a tent in the dark, while trying to placate hungry, car-tired children, isn't the best start to your holiday. Arriving just after lunch, perhaps having stopped for a picnic on the way, is ideal; you can then choose a lovely spot, get your camp sorted out and be cheffing up a tasty teatime treat by late afternoon. You might even be able to fit in a trip to the seaside/run through the woods/walk on the moor as well.

putting safety first

You'll probably find that your children will make friends, fast, with your site neighbours. Free from adult social hang-ups, kids will eye each other up and get stuck into a game of football pretty quickly. Make sure you've checked out the site beforehand, so that you are aware of any cliff-top paths or meandering streams, and know exactly how close the site is to the nearest road. We don't go in for huge municipal sites in this book, so if you're staying on a site listed here, we hope that it'll be a small, friendly site with lots of other children for yours to play with. Having said that, it's easy to lose sight of a child, quickly, between tents. Camping should give your kids a chance to push the boundaries a bit, in a safe environment, but the younger your kids are, the more nerve-wracking this can be. Knowing about potential hazards can help you relax and make you feel less of a headless chicken when you're squawking around the site trying to locate your kids for tea.

booking in time

While there's often spare space during the spring and autumn seasons, the days of turning up speculatively at a campsite in summer and expecting to find room are all but gone. In particular, given *Cool Camping*'s focus on smaller, independent campsites, many of those featured in this book fill up well in advance for the school holidays and the big bank holiday weekends. Almost all campsites take bookings over the phone

during regular working hours or you can visit the *Cool Camping* website (coolcamping.com) where you can select dates, check live availability and book online with the click of a button. So while you may be busy telling the kids to put down that iPad or turn off their phone, the digital world is good for one thing – getting a site booked early.

having wet-weather fun

We know that our great British weather can make or break a camping trip and we really hope that you're camping under glorious sunny skies, but if you aren't, don't despair, as certain strategies can help you cope. A bit of pre-trip research goes a long way. Be sure to check out the forecast before you leave and, if it's looking grim, gen up on local museums, castles, activity centres, swimming pools and cinemas. Once you're there, that extra bit of research will have been time well spent. Ask at the campsite, too, if certain restaurants are more accepting of wet, muddy children than others. If you're feeling energetic, just brave the rain and relish the fact that you can run around on an empty beach, where you would have been getting wet anyway.

keeping dry

One of the first rules of scouts is that in wet weather you must keep your top half dry and there's no need to worry about your legs. A mac over shorts and wellies is a good combo: long trousers stay wet all day, but skin dries in no time. It's always nice to make your tent cosy, but it's essential when the weather's grim. An extra blanket under sleeping bags will keep kids warmer than one on top, as cold comes up through the ground, and have a no-shoes rule in the tent. The last thing you want is to curl up in a sleeping bag coated with mud. It's also a good rule to keep one set of dry clothes for each child down their sleeping bag. And when packing, you can never take too many socks. But don't let rain spoil your fun; remember that your children probably mind about it a lot less than you do. Most children relish the anarchy of wet weather, and its mud-sliding opportunities.

cooking up a storm

Campfire cooking, or cooking on a barbecue, is one of the great delights of camping with kids. If you're lucky enough to find a site where you can have a fire (and, happily, there are lots about – see p10 for listings), educate your children to respect the flames. Children and fires are a dangerous combination, but part of the pleasure of camping is that it gives them a chance to learn practical skills that they might be missing in normal life. Lots of us don't have open fires at home, but being able to light and understand a proper fire is a handy life skill. Teach them to cook on that fire, and you might have a budding camp chef on your hands. But whether they are cooking mackerel or toasting marshmallows, teaching them how to respect a fire is a lot more useful than banning them from going anywhere near it. And there are few things more pleasurable in life than sitting round a glowing campfire with your kids, drinking mugs of steaming hot chocolate.

take a play tent?

Packing a football or rounders bat means you've always got a game handy for your children to occupy themselves with. Board games and cards are useful for wet weather, but fiddly little counters and pieces will quickly get lost. Wink murder (see p85) is much simpler, and it doesn't cost a penny. If your sleeping tent isn't capacious, why not take along a little extra tent for playing in, especially if your children are small? It can become a base for games and means that muddy children don't sit on top of their lovely dry, clean bedding. It also gives them a sense of having their own space and can easily become a Wendy house, space rocket or magic castle, depending on what mood they're in.

Most of all, just have fun. Camping is all about spending time together: cooking together, playing together and, at the end of the day, snuggling up together. It's that simple.

last but not least...

■ It's easy to forget... a water container, matches, towels, anoraks, tin openers, corkscrew, washing-up liquid and a sponge.
■ Camping will be easier with... fold-up chairs, wind-up torches, a chopping board, foil, a coolbox, chocolate.

Find and book your perfect camping holiday

To instantly check availability for hundreds of camping and glamping sites and book at the best price, visit

www.coolcamping.com

Blackberry Wood (p100)

trevalgan touring park

Trevalgan, St Ives, Cornwall TR26 3BJ 01736 791892 www.trevalgantouringpark.co.uk

Arrgh! There be pirates at this campsite. Ohh Arr, and there be farmers too. And, when you leave the imaginative playground, there be a fair number of beaches too!

Whether you're a bird, human or a semi-aquatic marine mammal, you will return to Trevalgan. Everyone does. This family-friendly site is a favourite summer spot for dolphins, seals and peace-loving campers, who not only fall in love with the dramatic north Cornwall coastline but also with Trevalgan Touring Park, too, which has a particularly welcoming feel. This is largely thanks to the owners Neil and Annette who, over the years, have given this site regular and well-deserved doses of TLC (not to mention investment) – modernising the facilities, adding homely touches and generally being on-hand to cheerfully dispense local knowledge.

Trevalgan's 135 pitches are only the kick of a beach ball from the Cornish coast, albeit a rather big kick! Campers have three options: non-serviced pitches that are ideal for basic camping; serviced spots, which include a 16-amp electric hook-up point; or fully serviced pitches that come complete with electricity, a fresh water tap and a water-drainage point. The majority of pitches are level, with defined access routes for vehicles. Yes, there may be a lot of caravans, but Trevalgan has plenty of space for kids to run free, while adults can easily find a quiet corner to kick back and enjoy the nearby coastal scenery.

And what scenery it is. Visitors can choose between safe bathing at Porthminster Beach (which inspired Virginia Woolf's novel *To the Lighthouse*) and award-winning Carbis Bay, where multiple operators offer first-time paddlers the chance to go sea-kayaking. Or there's Porthmeor, where surfers flock year after year for the world-class waves. The soft golden sand of this harbour beach is also popular with families, and it's a wonderful spot for puddle-jumping and splashing at low tide. On top of that, the chic holiday destination of St Ives is just 2 miles away from the site. Its quaint cobbled streets are home to a variety of interesting galleries, cafés and restaurants, all surrounded by miles of glorious beaches and crystal-clear waters.

With easy access to the rugged coastal footpath, secluded coves and numerous world-famous attractions (Land's End, The Minack Theatre and St Michael's Mount spring to mind), Trevalgan is ideally situated for families to explore the many delights of the Penwith peninsula. Youngsters may well, in years to come, remember this as the site where they fell in love with camping. It's that's sort of place.

WHO'S IN Tents, caravans, motorhomes, families, couples and dogs (maximum of 2) – yes. Groups – no.

ON SITE 135 grass pitches. Underfloor heated showers, family shower rooms, baby baths, disabled facilities, indoor dishwashing sinks, laundry room, chemical toilet disposal, gas exchange and freezers. Separate area for ball games, an excellent playground and well-equipped games room.

OFF SITE Wildlife lovers will enjoy a visit to Paradise Park (01736 751020), or you can get a taste of Cornish heritage at the nearby Geevor Tin Mine (01736 788662). Kayaking is a great way to explore the coast – Ocean Sports Centre (07533695031) on Carbis Bay caters for first-time paddlers. If you prefer someone else at the helm, the trip to Seal Island on The Dolly P (0777 300 8000) is not to be missed.

FOOD & DRINK The onsite shop stocks fresh bread and local produce, St Ives has a Co-op and there's a Tesco in Carbis Bay. Situated in St Ives harbour, The Lifeboat Inn (01736 794123) is a family-friendly pub serving food all day.

GETTING THERE Exit the A30 towards St Ives and take the first exit at the second mini roundabout, following the directions for 'St Ives (day visitors)'. At the T-junction turn right onto the B3311 and drive through Halsetown. Turn left at the next T-junction onto the B3306 towards St Just. After ½ mile turn right at the brown tourist sign. Follow this for ½ mile to a small triangle in the road; keep right and Trevalgan Touring Park is a short distance on the right.

PUBLIC TRANSPORT St Ives train station is less than 2 miles away; trains run to and from St Erth for connections on the Cornish main line. A regular bus service runs from the site to St Ives (timetables vary according to season) and takes dogs, pushchairs and surfboards.

OPEN April–October.

THE DAMAGE Non-serviced pitches (for 2 adults) £16–£31; serviced pitches (with 16amp electric hook-up) £21–£36; multi-serviced pitches (with electric hook-up, water and grey waste point) £23–£38; hard-standing multi-serviced pitches (with gravel base) £25–£40.

arthur's field

Treloan Lane, Gerrans, Portscatho, Truro, Cornwall TR2 5EF 01872 580989 www.coastalfarmholidays.co.uk

With three little beaches and a heritage farm just outside your tent, it's not hard to see why kids absolutely adore Arthur's Field. Just be ready for hissy fits at going-home time. Well, you can always come back next year.

You could call site owners Debbie and Peter Walker's relationship with Arthur's Field something of a love affair. And a pretty passionate one at that. When they first visited the site with their two young sons, to surf and explore the south coast at the point where Cornwall dips her heel into the dazzling waters of Falmouth Bay, the field was little more than a grassy farmer's paddock. One visit, though, and the Walkers were in love. The next time they arrived they were moving in.

Sitting on the clifftop just above Treloan Cove, and within strolling distance of postcard-pretty Portscatho, Arthur's Field is a site that stressed-out urbanite campers' dreams are made of. Certain things have changed since the rustic meadow of old but the place is far from overcome by Cornwall's summer tourist hordes, retaining that simple-but-effective campsite charm. Having pitched your tent, there's really no need to get into your car again until going-home time comes around. The problem is you may never want to go home at all. Just like Debbie and Peter, you'll end up wanting to live the dream.

Every person's dream is different, it must be said, and the couple have left ample room for each of their visitors to live out their own. They've crafted a site for all and the tents and caravans that were always welcoming visitors have recently been joined by a cosy eco-pod and yurt offering a host of seaside glamping comforts. Sandy buckets and spades are sometimes left idle as children abandon their beach plans to follow the sound of Debs' ringing bell, calling them to spend some time with the campsite's resident sheep, chickens and pigs, all of whom make this an authentic camping-on-the-farm experience. In the morning it's up to the little ones to collect freshly laid eggs and, by doing so, they get to meet the site's other families, By evening, when you reconvene around the fireside for one of the site's famous weekly social events, firm friends have already been made. Between the campsite, the beaches, the animals and the friends, the only downside at Arthur's Field is plain for all to see. Taking the kids home can be a tricky business, and since the Walkers aren't going anywhere, we are afraid that you can't move in. Best make plans for next year instead.

PLEASE SLOW

...and relax

WHO'S IN Tents, campervans, caravans, dogs – yes.

ON SITE 57 pitches, all with hook-up, plus a snug eco-pod and glamping yurt are also available. There are 11 showers (including 3 family showers) and 6 sinks (including 1 at child height). BBQs are permitted in trays. There are eggs to be collected and rabbits to pet, a football meadow to play in and cricket stumps to borrow. The site is also within walking distance of the cliffs, which is nice – but little ones should always be accompanied.

OFF SITE There is private access to no fewer than 3 secluded beaches, all of which are great for swimming, fishing and diving, especially Treloan Cove and Peter's Splosh. Slightly further afield are Carne and Towan beaches, both well worth the trip for their golden sands. Porthcurnick Beach is also walkable from the other side of Portscatho and seals are regular visitors. There are also several local castles to visit, including Caerhays Castle (01872 501310), Pendennis Castle (01326 316594) and St Mawes Castle (01326 270526).

FOOD & DRINK The Walkers organise a family evening twice a week. Simon, from the famous Hidden Hut on Porthcurnick Beach, comes to cook paella and other more local dishes, and a pizza van and chip van also come on occasional evenings. The Plume of Feathers (01872 580321) and The Royal Standard (01872 580271) are within walking distance – locally caught fish lifts their menus above standard pub grub. The Boathouse (01872 580326), in the village, is nice for cream teas.

GETTING THERE Follow the A3078 until you reach Trewithian. Turn left at 'Treloan Coastal Farm' towards Gerrans and Portscatho. Stay on this road until you reach Gerrans and stop beside the church, opposite the Royal Standard Inn. Treloan Lane is marked on the wall and runs directly to Arthur's Field, 300m down on the left.

OPEN All year.

THE DAMAGE Camping pitches £15–£25; the snug pod costs £33–£38 per night, the yurt from £40 per night.

tregarton park

Gorran, Nr Mevagissey, St Austell, Cornwall PL26 6NF 01726 843666 www.tregarton.co.uk

Old-world agricultural charms married with modern, high-tech facilities. You could camp with old grandpa and the tiniest of kiddies and they'd both be in their element here. It's like a camping holiday for the winners of The Generation Game.

Let's not beat around the tent pegs here; at first glance, Tregarton Park should be everything *Cool Camping* is not. Touring caravans are welcomed, pitches come well manicured and there's a distinct 'holiday park' vibe that may ruffle some traditional camping feathers. But as you pitch next to a 17th-century, grade-II-listed farm building, with coast and countryside views a-plenty, you soon realise that this is truly a cool place to camp after all.

The sprawling Tregarton Estate was built back in 1492 and is today run by the Hicks family, who remain determined to maintain the site's old-style charm. The walls have been constructed using traditional Cornish hedging methods and the paving areas are laid with natural, local slabs – granite, limestone and sandstone. Facilities, however, are anything but dated, with motion-sensor-operated showers, excellent access for the disabled and Wi-Fi all making for a proper 21st-century camping experience. As for things to do, there are lovely nearby beaches, including family friendly Porthluney Cove, as well as the Eden Project and Lost Gardens of Heligan – and scenic Fowey is not far away either.

So, if you're an 'old school' camper who still thinks caravans, Wi-Fi and other-worldly attractions just aren't cricket, then rest assured: you'll be too enthralled by Cornwall's tiny fishing ports and beautiful beaches to care.

WHO'S IN Tents, trailer tents, caravans, motorhomes, families, couples and dogs (max 2) – yes. Groups – no.

ON SITE 125 hedged pitches (divided into 4 meadows) all with electric hook-ups; 31 hardstanding pitches (some with sea views); 1 toilet/shower block with disabled facilities. Laundry room, park shop and takeaway, playground, tennis court, heated outdoor pool and recreational area.

OFF SITE Tregarton is situated less than 2 miles from Porthluney Cove, a sandy and secluded, family-friendly beach. While there, visit nearby Caerhays Castle (01872 501310), whose 100 acres of woodland host England's largest collection of magnolias. Scenic Fowey has an impressive maritime history, and the ferry crossing from picturesque Mevagissey is a lovely way to get there.

FOOD & DRINK The site has a summer takeaway service, and lunches and early evening meals are available by the pool. Lobbs Farm Shop (01726 844411) has great local produce, and fresh fish can be bought on the harbour in Mevagissey. The local pub, The Barley Sheaf (01726 843330), a mile away in Gorran, offers excellent homemade food, as does the Llawnroc Hotel (01726 843461) 2 miles further on.

GETTING THERE Leave St Austell on the B3273, go through Pentewan; at the crossroads at the top of the hill, follow the signs to the Lost Gardens of Heligan and Gorran Haven.

PUBLIC TRANSPORT The nearest train station is St Austell (7 miles away); the closest bus stop is at the Lost Gardens of Heligan, 2 miles away.

OPEN March–October.

THE DAMAGE Tent (including 2 people) and electric hook-up £8–£32 per night.

trewan hall

St Columb, Cornwall TR9 6DB 01637 880261 www.trewan-hall.co.uk

When your children have grown up, all their most cherished memories of making new friends, playing games and splashing in a summer swimming pool will revolve around this campsite. But only if you take them there, of course.

The 36 acres of undulating fields, immaculate gardens and enchanting woodland that surrounds the 17th-century manor house of Trewan Hall, make for a near-perfect camping spot. Positioned just outside the pretty small town of St Columb Major, this family-orientated campsite has been run by the Hill family for over 50 years, so it's fair to say they know a thing or two about camping. And with Cornwall's finest walks, pristine white sand beaches and picture-postcard villages right on the site's doorstep, you don't have to be a genius to work out what brought them here in the first place – and, for that matter, why they have never left.

Trewan's camping area itself is lovely, and small enough to feel quite private, with two slightly sloping fields – one smaller and more family-friendly and a larger field with plenty of space and a real 'away from it all' atmosphere. The management here is flexible about where you go, and campers can pitch where they like, so if a secluded corner takes your fancy, it's yours! Not being slap-bang on the Cornish coast means the site is also relatively sheltered from the elements. It's worth mentioning that a country lane runs alongside the smaller camping field, but unless you're an extremely light sleeper you won't be disturbed by the infrequent traffic.

Caravans and motorhomes are also welcome at Trewan Hall. But fret not, canvas campers: given the site's pursuit of natural beauty over profit, the grass-only pitches and absence of hard-standings mean only a relatively small number of caravans take their chances, so the comprehensive views of rolling fields, parish churches and grass-munching cattle remain largely unbroken. The facilities here are pretty comprehensive too, with a brand-new ablution block equipped with showers, baths, washing-up sinks and electric razor points. Best of all, guests are free to use the fully supervised, 25-metre heated swimming pool (which is open during high season; 60p per visit) – just the ticket for cooling off when the Cornish sun comes out to play.

You won't have a shortage of things to do here. Not only do you have the nearby historic town of St Columb Major, with its selection of time-honoured country pubs; you're also just a flip-flop away from the tranquil coastline at Mawgan Porth, and just 14 miles down the road is the world's largest and most impressive greenhouse, The Eden Project. These sights, combined with the cosy, grassy comfort that comes with field camping, make Trewan Hall an ideal place to pitch up.

WHO'S IN Tents, caravans, campervans, families, couples and well-behaved dogs – yes. Young groups – no.

ON SITE Around 200 pitches across 2 fields. Well-equipped wash-block with family rooms, disabled access, hairdryers and wetsuit washing areas. A fully stocked shop, library/writing room, plus a supervised 25m heated swimming pool (60p a visit). Various barns available for table tennis, table football, pool and darts. Basketball area in the barnyard, comprehensive woodland playground for children including a sandpit and a large, open field for football and other games. Regular entertainment in various forms includes a magician, rock bands, animal shows and story-telling.

OFF SITE The nearby Eden Project (01726 811911) is one millennium project that's been a success, while the flat, easygoing Camel Trail is the result of more recent funding, starting in Padstow and running east through Wadebridge (along the Camel Estuary) before finishing at Poley's Bridge. The Padstow–Wadebridge section makes a splendid half-day excursion, but it does get crowded. The Wadebridge–Bodmin section is usually quieter and just as dramatic. Bikes can be hired from both ends.

FOOD & DRINK Hot food, including great pasties, is available all day in the campsite shop. There's also a fish & chip van and a pizza 'horse box' that visit once a week. Within walking distance, St Columb Major has several places to eat, including Port Starboard (01726 860270), where they serve up great fish and chips, the atmospheric Ring O'Bells (01637 880259) and Goss Moor Tea Garden (01726 861113), which has well-presented and reasonably priced cakes and sandwiches.

GETTING THERE From the A39, turn off when you see the signs for St Eval Talskiddy and follow the road for ¾ mile. You will see the site entrance on your right.

OPEN Mid May–mid September.

THE DAMAGE Adults £7–£12, children (3–15yrs) £3.50–£6.60. Electric hook-ups £6. Dogs £2. Extra cars £2.

ruthern valley holidays

Ruthern Bridge, Bodmin, Cornwall PL30 5LU 01208 831395 www.ruthernvalley.com

Cornwall isn't all about sun, sand and surfing. What about rabbits, woodpeckers, squirrels and trees? Woody, green Ruthern feels a million miles from the bustling Cornish coast, but it's actually only a short drive away.

After a nice day on the beach at Polzeath or Rock, surrounded by surfers and Sloanes, Ruthern Valley is somewhere to escape to, hidden amid the green canopy of the Cornish countryside. Spread among a band of trees and skirted by small streams that ultimately feed the nearby River Camel, this secluded, beguiling little site is humming with wildlife. Children can have plenty of fun spotting rabbits and squirrels, and budding ornithologists can look out out for woodpeckers a-pecking and hear owls a-hooting. Having said that, they'll probably enjoy feeding the chickens just as much.

The campsite occupies a top location, too, with the wild delights of Bodmin Moor close at hand – the perfect place for stomping around with children, as you regale them with heady stories of smugglers and highwaymen. Or you could cycle to Padstow for a crabbing session on the quay and perhaps a slap-up portion of Mr Stein's famous fish and chips, which is a pretty much perfect way to while away an afternoon. Nearby Grogley Woods, is also lovely for shady walks. Then, at the end of a busy day, when you've had your fill of sun, sea and sand, what could be better than the peaceful, leafy shade of Ruthern Valley?

WHO'S IN Tents, campervans, caravans – yes. Dogs – no.

ON SITE 16 meadow pitches and 4 more secluded pitches in the woods. Some electric hook-ups. Wigwams (sleeping 5), camping pods (sleeping 4) and timber lodge holiday homes also available. 4 solar-powered showers, 2 washing-up sinks and laundry facilities include 2 washers, 2 dryers and an ironing board. Bicycle hire. See website for glamping details.

OFF SITE Part of the appeal of Ruthern Valley is its proximity to the Camel Trail, a disused railway track running 16 miles from Wadebridge to Padstow; a great route for walking or cycling. Hire bikes from the site to take it on.

FOOD & DRINK There's a small site shop for basic groceries and local produce. Cycle 3 miles along the Camel Trail to the Borough Arms (01208 731118), a child-friendly pub.

GETTING THERE Follow the A30 past Bodmin to Innis Downs and the roundabout for St Austell. Turn right, taking you back over the A30 to the next roundabout and take the second exit signed for Lanivet (A389). Pass through Lanivet until you see Presingoll Pottery on the left. Turn left, signed Nanstallon; turn left again, signed Ruthern Bridge and continue for about 2 miles, turning left immediately before the small bridge.

PUBLIC TRANSPORT Bus sightings are rarer than those of the Beast of Bodmin Moor, so catch a train to Bodmin Parkway and take a taxi. Or bring your bike, jump on the steam train to Boscarne on the Camel Trail and pedal to Grogley Halt – a mile's level cycle from the site.

OPEN All year.

THE DAMAGE From £12.50 per tent for 2 adults plus £4 for children; wigwams £45–£60 a night; camping pods £30–£35.

cornish tipi holidays

Tregildrans Quarry, Trelill, St Kew, Cornwall PL30 3HZ 01208 880781 www.cornishtipiholidays.co.uk

So this is what happens when nature takes back control! You'd never know there was an old quarry here, now hidden under a serene, spring-fed lake that's so beautiful you want to jump straight in. Don't worry. Nobody's stopping you.

Rural Cornwall doesn't exactly strike you as a place ahead of the curve. Take this campsite, for instance. Arranged around a stunning spring-fed lake in the old Tregildrans Quarry, it has an altogether more timeless quality. The thick, mature trees, emerald waters and fern-covered escarpments that tumble down into the lake could well have been painted many centuries ago. There's no onsite shop taking contactless payment cards, no Wi-Fi, no playground. It's all a bit archaic. Isn't it?

In fact, few campsites are as ahead of the curve as Cornish Tipi Holidays. Back when we first discovered the site in our first edition of *Cool Camping: Kids*, 'CTH', as the campsite sometimes calls itself, had already been running for 10 years and was championing something innovative. Set up in 1996 by Elizabeth Tom, it was the first commercial tipi campsite in England, offering nights beneath the stars in a tipi before the word 'glamping' had even been invented. Today the 25 North American-style abodes are still going strong, with three different sizes on offer, but have been joined by regular camping too – a new twist in the CTH story.

While fashionistas are throwing up Alice Temperley-style tipis and yurts across the great British countryside, Cornish Tipi Holidays, ever ahead of the game, are part of the new back-to-basics culture. Bring your own tent, avoid the crowds and pick whatever pitch you want – choosing from an open meadow space with fellow campers, a private clearing among the trees, a grassy patch with views… there's a full 20 acres of space to explore, so you're sure to find a spot to suit you.

All of these campers have the same facilities as the tipi dwellers – hot showers and loos – while the campsite environment lends itself wholeheartedly to anyone with an imagination. It's easy to spend entire days by the lake, messing about in a boat or fishing for trout (bring your own rods and licence; lifejackets can be borrowed from the warden). You can even bring your own canoe if you really want to. Playing hide and seek along the winding paths edged by fat blackberries or bright yellow gorse is a must, while there's also the larger 'village field' for children to charge about in, and the 'top village field' with its spectacular totem pole. In this wilder-than-wild environment, kids can't fail to flourish. No surprise, then, to hear that Alice Temperley herself spent her honeymoon here. Now what on earth would Hiawatha have thought about that?

WHO'S IN Glampers, campers, tents, campervans, caravans, couples, families, kids, groups, weddings – yes. Dogs – no.

ON SITE Camping pitches and 25 tipis (11 tipis together for groups in the 'village field'). Loos and showers at either end of the site, plus an additional, larger shower block. Every tipi has a lantern and box of utensils, along with rugs and a few furnishings. Water taps around the site. Paths, streams, lake and woodland to explore, boats and lifejackets to borrow. Fishing is popular, as is cooking the catch on a campfire – though stick to the firepit areas provided and use the cleverly recycled horseshoe trivets for cooking.

OFF SITE It's a 5-minute drive to some of the best sea-kayaking, stand-up paddleboarding and adrenaline-filled coasteering in the UK – all out of beautiful Port Quin. Try Cornish Coast Adventures (01209 880280) for routes and equipment. Or head to Port Isaac, also a great place for sea-kayaking and for buying the freshest scallops or crabs. If you've brought your bikes (or fancy renting some) you should pick up the Camel Trail near Wadebridge and explore what John Betjeman described as 'the best journey in England'.

FOOD & DRINK An onsite café serves breakfasts, lunches, freshly baked pizzas and homemade cakes. For groceries use the Co-op in Port Isaac. You can buy excellent pasties from either Aunt Avice at St Kew (01208 841895) or Cornish Maids in Camelford (01840 212749). Rick Stein's fish & chips (01841 532700) on the quay at Padstow are unbeatable, with everything from cod, to battered oysters, to St Ives' calamari.

GETTING THERE Take the M5 to Exeter, then the A30 to Launceston. Turn right onto the A395. Just before Camelford turn right at Collan's Cross onto the B3314 to Delabole; 2 miles after Delabole turn left for St Teath at the Port Gaverne crossroads. After the old railway bridge, take the first right before Normansland Cottage.

OPEN Easter–early October.

THE DAMAGE Wild camping from £18 per adult, £9 per child. A family of up to 5 in a large tipi £660–£980 per week with a min stay of 2 nights. Includes all boats, fishing, swimming etc.

enchanted valley yurts

Tregrove Farm, Lanreath, Looe, Cornwall PL13 2NY 01503 220880 www.enchantedvalleyyurts.co.uk

Campfires. Stargazing from bed. Home comforts under canvas. No wonder yurts are the accommodation of choice in Outer Mongolia. And with an exotic wildlife park on the doorstep, this site could be in a foreign land too, were it not for the British weather.

There's something ever so right about describing this valley as 'enchanting'. The sound of the stream that bubbles its way through the 34-acre smallholding ranges from gurgling to an almost silent trickling when the weather is dry. The long grasses change from a buttercup-speckled yellow in June to a light, sun-scorched green by August. And the trees, hedges and saplings are as inviting to children as any artificial playground. It's a wonderful place to explore and the two yurts here have been fittingly finished to provide the same enchanting feel. Solar-powered fairy lights and lanterns cast their ambient light across the exposed wooden lattice on the inside of each structure, while wood-burning stoves and colour-schemed furnishings give a warm and cosy feel. They are, of course, also perfectly practical. Each yurt sleeps up to six people – saving space with the use of foldaway futons – and is accompanied by a neighbouring cabin with your own private shower and toilet facilities. The mown grass provides children with a space to play and also leads you to a communal log cabin that's home to the main kitchen and dining area. It comes complete with

everything you need (including a range cooker) plus there's an outside cooking area with a proper pizza oven and a campfire.

Owl yurt is perhaps the more secluded of the two, across the stream beyond a line of bushes and accessed by way of a tiny bridge, while Pheasant yurt is closer to the kitchen area. When the sun's out, it's all so nice that it's difficult to leave. The raised wooden platforms on which each yurt sits have outdoor furniture where you can sit and enjoy a sundowner and even put your feet up and relax under the guise of 'supervising the kids'. They'll be keen to wander off to find the horses and llamas grazing the meadows just around the corner. Don't worry, they're a very friendly bunch.

Enchanting though it may be, there is life beyond the valley, and once you drag yourself away you'll be quick to realise that the coast is a major draw here. Fantastic beaches and the charming harbour town of Looe await, stacked up along the steep sides of the river valley, just a 15-minute drive away. From Looe you can chug out on the ferry to the nature reserve of Looe Island or join the coastal path to wander to neighbouring coves and beaches.

WHO'S IN Glamping only. Tents, caravans, dogs – no.

ON SITE Two yurts, each sleeping 5–6 people, furnished with a double bed, day beds, futons (bedding provided) and a wood-burning stove. Table, chairs and chimenea on the outer deck. Shared kitchen with a range cooker, hobs, electric oven, microwave, toaster, kettle, cutlery and crockery, tables and chairs, fridge and freezer. Outside dining tent with a bench table and further cooking area with a pizza oven, BBQ and campfire area. Private shower and flushing toilet facilities.

OFF SITE You can walk to Porfell Wildlife Park (01503 220211), a sanctuary with exotic animals from around the world, or visit the Monkey Sanctuary (01503 262532) just the other side of Looe – an atmospheric home to rescued monkeys set atop cliffs with beautiful views and gardens. Alternatively, head to Bodmin Moor for more challenging walking routes and some native British wildlife.

FOOD & DRINK The closest pub to the campsite is The Jubilee Inn (01503 220312) at Pelynt, which serves excellent food, while The Rashleigh Inn ('the inn on the beach'; 01726 813991) at Polkerris has the best views. For everyday supplies, Lanreath has a community shop and post office within walking distance, although up a steep hill. There's also a Spar in Pelynt, a Co-op in Looe or major supermarkets in Liskeard and Bodmin.

GETTING THERE At the end of the M5, join the A38 to Plymouth and continue to Liskeard. At the end of the dual carriageway, follow the signs to St Austell on the A390 to East Taphouse and turn left to Looe. Continue on the B3359 towards Lanreath and, just before the village, turn right to Polruan. Follow this for 500m. The campsite is down the lane to your right.

OPEN Easter–October. Check in before dark.

THE DAMAGE From £295 per yurt (Mon–Fri or Fri–Mon) or £530 for the week.

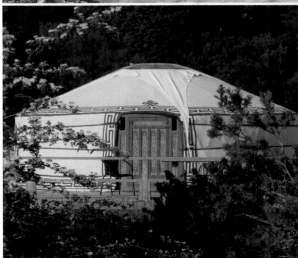

cerenety eco camping

Lower Lynstone Lane, Bude, Cornwall EX23 0LR 07429 016962 www.cerenetycampsite.co.uk

'Happy eco camping' brags the tagline. And happy is just what you'll feel here if you're eco-minded and wild about camping. Just a short walk from the kiss-me-quick seaside at Bude, Cerenety is all about being green and taking it easy.

In the eyes of the wild-camping tribes, campsites are for softies. But wild camping with kids – well, it can just be a bit of a hassle. At the very least it's nice to know there's running water to deal with potty mishaps and stacks of dirty dishes. With its no-frills, close-to-nature approach, Cerenety proves you can still enjoy the wilder side of camping on a regular campsite.

First and foremost, with the majority of the grassy fields left empty, even in the summer, across Cerenety's seven sprawling acres, there's plenty of space to run around like wild things. Every feature is as squeaky green as the surrounding countryside, from compost loos and solar panels to recycled materials ingeniously put to use in the site's rustic, efficient amenities. There's even a veggie patch and a permaculture forest garden, where you can pick your own and have a forage.

Children also flock to bottle-feed orphan lambs, and alpacas roam a few feet shy of the tents. Where nature rules and campfire smoke spirals lazily into dusky skies, it comes as a surprise that the surfer dudes, amusement arcades and retro cafés of Bude are just a mile's easy stroll along the canal. So kids can get a seaside fix without you having to hunt down the car keys. Once they've hit the waves, gorged on ice cream and hired a pedalo, you might even experience a rare moment of serenity when they rest their tired little heads back at Cerenety Eco Camping.

WHO'S IN Groups, small campervans, tents, dogs (by arrangement) – yes. Caravans, large campervans – no.

ON SITE 3 sprawling fields with no set pitches. A field shelter houses 2 showers, 3 compost loos and 2 washing-up sinks. Owner Jake will freeze iceblocks for you in the house, if you ask. A small shop sells basics. Pick your own veggies from the patch, explore the forest garden and enjoy the wildlife pond. Feed the orphan lambs and pet the animals – Flipper the dog, Torry the pony and Red the rescue horse, as well as alpacas, rabbits, ducks and chickens. Campfires and BBQs encouraged.

OFF SITE It's a 5-minute stroll to the campsite's 'secret beach' or a 20-minute walk to Bude's stunning Summerleaze, Crooklets and Widemouth beaches, which serve up a heady cocktail of surf, sand and cool waterfront cafés. Hit the waves with Raven Surf School (01288 353693) or Big Blue Surf School (01288 331764), or row a boat along the canal (boat hire at Lower Wharf: 07968 688782).

FOOD & DRINK Walk to Bude for options; the nearest family friendly pub is The Brendon Arms (01288 354542; ¾ mile).

GETTING THERE Bascially head for Bude and at the mini roundabout where you would turn right for the town centre, go straight across towards Widemouth Bay. Follow the road over the bridge and up the hill. At the top, turn left opposite Upper Lynstone Caravan Park and follow the lane to the end. Turn right at the T-junction. The campsite is on the right.

PUBLIC TRANSPORT Get the train or bus to Exeter, then get the bus (6 or 6A) from Exeter to Bude. From Plymouth, the number 12 is a direct bus to Cerenety.

OPEN March–October.

THE DAMAGE From £4–£10 per person per night.

bales ash

Bales Ash, High Bickington, Nr Umberleigh, Devon EX37 9BL 01769 561063 www.balesash.co.uk

Summer comes and summer goes but the memories from this pop-up paradise will stick with little ones forever. If every empty meadow could be transformed in this way, then the world would surely be a better place.

Like all the best campsites, there's not much to see at Bales Ash for most of the year. It has a quietly ephemeral feel that almost makes you wonder whether a campsite really calls this patch of Devon's Taw Valley home at all. There's no playground and just a few faint lines traced in the grass by vehicles that disappeared in mid-September. But summer is an altogether different story. Alive with tents and infused by the sound of children's laughter, the distant strumming of a guitar and the evocative aroma of smouldering barbecues, the campsite is perfect entirely because of its lack of all things permanent. This is a lesson in how all campsites should be: pop-up, fuss-free, sheep-mown aprons of grass that are refreshingly understated.

Camping at Bales Ash is very much of the chilled-out variety. There are a handful of electric hook-ups for small campervans that don't mind the country lanes, and two spacious fields where up to 30 families or groups can spread themselves around. After that, it's up to you to find the excitement, whether it's with impromptu games of football or communal evening campfires where kiddies gorge themselves on marshmallows. That said, animal lovers will enjoy checking in with the rabbits in 'The Bunny House' opposite the shower block, while parents and young children alike will revel in Hungry Gorilla's Story Tent where a friendly life-sized gorilla (don't worry – he's stuffed!) takes up residence for the summer with a selection of children's books for you to enjoy.

Yet, for all its simplicity, Bales Ash still has everything you could possibly need. Camp firepits are rented out at just £3 for your entire stay, high-spec hot showers and top-notch compost toilets are available for use and there's even Wi-Fi. It's the very antithesis of the holiday park scene, right down to the beautifully furnished bell tents (aka 'The Belles of Bales Ash') nestled against the hedge in the small field – perfect if you seek a bit of luxury and don't fancy putting up your own tent. And while we're talking about luxury, why not treat yourself to one of Ann, Debbie and Caro's unbeatable cream teas while enjoying the view from outside their Victorian summer house shop and café?

Beyond, views over the hedges to Exmoor may draw you out from your camping cocoon. It's a half-hour drive to the national park, though footpaths closer to home offer similarly pleasant routes. To the north, Barnstaple and the coast are closer still and boast some of the best surfing beaches in the country. By the time winter comes back around you'll never look at an empty field the same way again.

WHO'S IN Tents, campervans, awnings and event shelters, dogs – yes. Large caravans and motorhomes – no.

ON SITE 30 pitches and 3 fully equipped 5m bell tents. 3 showers, 3 compost toilets, electric hook-ups, water taps in both fields, washing machine and freezer. Free Wi-Fi. Campfires in firepits, plus a large communal firepit.

OFF SITE The campsite has direct access to a number of local walks – try the gentle 1-hour route to the pubs in High Bickington or visit the woods at Kingford Hill, owned by the Woodland Trust. Saunton, Croyde, Woolacombe, and Putsborough are the best-known local beaches and are all within a 30-minute drive. They're awash with places where you can rent surfboards or take lessons.

FOOD & DRINK Homemade cream teas are available onsite, along with basic provisions, fresh farm eggs and home-baked cakes. There is a well-stocked community shop in the village, while nearby Barnstaple has all the shops you need for further supplies. There are 2 pubs in High Bickington, a pleasant 20-minute walk from the campsite: The Golden Lion (01769 561006) – a 19th-century haunt with a single bar and grainy local pictures from yesteryear; and The Old George Inn (01769 560513), a thatched local from the 1500s that retains many original features. Both serve good food.

GETTING THERE From the A377 at Kingford, follow the signs for High Bickington up the mile-long Kingford Hill. Near the top you pass holiday lodge signs and then a skid warning sign on your left. Immediately after, follow a blue arrow sign to Bales Ash on your right. Proceed up the lane for a ¼ mile. The campsite entrance is through a metal gate on your left.

PUBLIC TRANSPORT The nearest train stations are Umberleigh (4 miles) or Portsmouth Arms (1½ miles; tell the conductor you want to get off there or they won't stop!). Pick-up can often be arranged if needed.

OPEN Late May–early September.

THE DAMAGE £8 per person per night, £4 per child (4–16yrs), under-4s free.

westland farm

Bratton Fleming, Barnstaple, Devon EX31 4SH 01598 763301 www.westlandfarm.co.uk

What kind of farmer does your child want to be? A shepherd in his hut? A drover in her cabin? A farmer in his farmhouse? Or a, ummm, Mongolian in his yurt? There are all sorts of accommodation here and they'll all make your little farmers happy.

For city-dwelling campers especially, there are few things that bring the reality of camping home as much as taking a stroll through a dewy early morning field to use a shower block. Pausing to inhale the clear air, still scented with the smoky fragrance of last night's campfire, while watching the mist rising off the rolling fields, even the most jaded urbanite can't fail to be stirred.

Westland Farm is the perfect place for such epiphanies: a beautifully tranquil glampsite that looks out over a small lake surrounded by rolling, sheep-dotted hills. There's a variety of accommodation, too, ranging from pitches in a lush, grassy field to a brilliant shepherd's hut set in a quiet corner at the top of the farm. Close to the loos and showers, and nestled next to a babbling brook, the hut comes complete with a 5ft double bed and a bunkbed and airbed for small children (if you need them) – perfect for a family of four. Then there's the giant yurt that comfortably sleeps six and a hand-built, grass-roofed Drover's Hut (sleeping a further six), with a kitchen that houses a wood-fired oven and gas hob, set in its own private corner of a field next to the stream. You can even snag a B&B room in the farmhouse if the outdoor life is not for you. A beautiful spot, and perfect for both a romantic getaway and a family escape from the urban jungle.

WHO'S IN Everyone, really. Tents, campervans, caravans, dogs (although not in the yurt), all kinds of groups – yes.

ON SITE Shepherd's Hut, Yurt, Drover's Hut, plus 5 pitches; clean washrooms with 2 toilets and 2 showers, fridge/freezer, mobile-charging point and fresh eggs available from the farm's hens. Kids can also help feed the horses or lambs. Campfires allowed (in firepits).

OFF SITE Exmoor Zoo (01598 76332) is close by, as is Combe Martin Wildlife and Dinosaur Park (01271 882486). The seaside towns of Ilfracombe, Lynton and Lynemouth all offer plenty to explore.

FOOD & DRINK The Black Venus Inn (01598 763251) in Challacombe, a 5-minute drive away, has superb home-cooked food in nice surroundings. The Old Station Inn (01598 763520) at Blackmoor Gate is also worth a look. The Pyne Arms (01271 850055) at East Down offers locally produced food, some supplied by Westland Farm itself. If you're looking to self-cater, check out Barnstaple's indoor Pannier Market (01271 379084), offering fresh local goods, flowers, crafts and more.

GETTING THERE Head down the A39 in North Devon, setting the sat nav for EX31 4SH. Keep the speed down because it's easy to miss the farm's sign when you're close.

OPEN All year.

THE DAMAGE Camping £8 per person per night. Shepherd's hut from £75 per night. Yurt from £95 per night for up to 4 people. Drover's hut from £95 per night. Extra people, camping or staying in the yurt £7 per person per night. Children half the adult fee. Under-4s free.

kingsmead centre

Kingsmead Centre, Clayhidon, Devon EX15 3TR 01823 421630 www.kingsmeadcentre.com

Recharge your fading batteries by plugging into some woodland relaxation. You'll find a sprinkling of campfire magic plus a handy dose of lakeside chilling will do the trick. It's the perfect remedy.

A campsite that caters for everyone is a difficult thing to find, and it's fair to say that not everyone gets it right. Providing the luxury of high-end glamping, the off-grid natural atmosphere for campers and hard-standing spaces for caravans is always a tricky mix. But there are one or two places that pull it all off seamlessly. The Kingsmead Centre, on the border of Devon and Somerset, is just such a site, where everyone you meet wears the grin of utter contentment. Here there truly is something for everyone and, with only a few precious spots available, it's a site to snap up fast, however you choose to stay.

Divided into a top and bottom field, the seven sloping acres of meadowy heathland boast a toilet block at either end of the gradient. In the lower field are open, well-spaced pitches that leave room for kids to play. Harder ground can be found in the upper field, along with electrified spots for caravans and campers. Some of the best areas, though, are found by delving into the woods and pitching a tent in one of the natural clearings dotted about – a real slice of wilderness within an already beautiful campsite.

Glampers hoping to arrive with just a toothbrush and their jim-jams are also in luck. There's a parked-up showman's caravan (more of the modern-day traveller's kind than the horse-drawn type of old) decked from head to toe like a furnished, self-catered home. There's

a furnished Lily Pad Belle Tent, which is tall enough for parents to stand up in. And there's also a spectacular yurt, set in its own woodland glade. The lattice-work of the traditional structure is wonderfully exposed inside, while the light, cream canvas gives it an airy outdoor feel.

Along the lower end of the campsite, what we have named 'the woods' are, in fact, a shielding flank of trees that hide away another of the campsite's features. Following a footpath beneath the canopy, it's a 30-metre walk to the first of two fishing lakes, built for the exclusive use of Kingsmead Centre. Rod licences are cheaply and easily available from the post office, so the lakes offer a good chance for families to try casting their very first fishing line. The lakes are also surrounded by forestry commission land and colourful wildflower meadows, and footpaths and bridleways stretch into the beautiful Blackdown Hills – top territory for walkers, cyclists and equestrians. If you're particularly keen you can even bring along your own horse and graze it in the neighbouring field!

All in all the campsite exudes a warm, family-friendly atmosphere that reflects the welcoming personalities of hosts Tristan and Jodie (along with Pickles the dog). The site is also brilliantly placed for all the delights of this part of Devon, with beaches within easy driving distance, a cluster of pleasant market towns and a host of excellent village pubs.

WHO'S IN Everyone! Tents, caravans, motorhomes, campervans, glampers, campers, families, couples, dogs.

ON SITE Grass pitches, a handful of hardstandings and tent-only pitches in the woods. There is also a modern showman's caravan, a Lotus Pad Belle Tent and a yurt in the woods. There are 2 toilet and shower blocks, including a new wash-block that will make you re-think your idea of what 'roughing it' means, with spacious family bathrooms and a washing-up room with fridge and tourist information. Campfires allowed in firepits only. 2 fishing lakes.

OFF SITE Explore the rest of the Blackdown Hills Area of Outstanding Natural Beauty by foot, bike or on horseback. The site has maps and leaflets available explaining the best routes nearby and Jodie and Tristan are also a wealth of local knowledge. By car the coast is naturally a popular destination with top beaches within a 45-minute drive, while Knightshays Court (01884 254665), Bickleigh Castle (01884 855363) and Killerton (01392 881345) offer some grand local history.

FOOD & DRINK 2 miles away, the Half Moon Inn (01823 680291) is a good choice and a pleasant walk from the campsite, while The Holman Clavel in Culmhead (01823 421070) hosts a great range of locallymade ales and their very own 'Tricky' Cider.

GETTING THERE Entering the postcode in a sat nav doesn't often work, so use written directions. Leave the M5 at junction 26 and follow the A38 south to Wellington. At the staggered crossroads follow the brown tourist sign for The Merry Harriers and continue to the top of the hill where the Kingsmead Centre is signposted left. Continue to the Merry Harriers pub and turn right. The site entrance is ¼ mile down this road on the left.

OPEN All year, weather permitting (call to check in winter).

THE DAMAGE Pitches from £15 per night for 2 people. Additional adults £5; additional children (4–16yrs) £2.50; under-4s free. See website for glamping prices.

moorhouse campsite

Moorhouse Farm, Holford, Bridgwater, Somerset TA5 1SP 01278 741295 www.moorhousecampsite.co.uk

Moorhouse would make the perfect setting for a Famous Five story. The surrounding Quantocks offer hearty hill walking, there are streams for afternoon tea picnics and there's a good rock-pooling beach nearby for scooping up hidden treasure. Mischievous adventures await.

Moorhouse Campsite is pinned between hills and coastline, just 200m away from a busy road yet boasting an undeniably enviable location. Characterised by the rocky Jurassic Coast, heather-coated hills and long, wooded valleys, the surrounding Quantock Hills are magnificent to explore. It was such local beauty that inspired a young William Wordsworth and his friend Samuel Taylor Coleridge, to pen many of the poems in *Lyrical Ballads* – a book that is often held to mark the beginning of English literary Romanticism. More than two centuries on, the surroundings that roused them are just as inspirational.

Located on a working arable farm, Moorhouse is a quiet, family-run site that boasts far-reaching views across this very landscape to the climbing hills beyond. There's a range of options when it comes to pitches, with seasonal, hardstanding and tent pitches all on offer, each carefully spaced out and divided by maturing trees and hedges. The rich foliage provides not only privacy but also some extra shade for lucky summer campers, and shelter from the rain for unlucky ones. If you're really worried about the weather, though, there are also two glamping pods for a little added luxury, kitted out with simple beds and mattresses – ideal if you don't fancy pitching the tent.

Onsite facilities are numerous. Two conveniently placed toilet blocks mean that late-night expeditions will never be too tasking, and a single, centrally located shower block boasts wonderfully powerful showers. Laundry facilities are also available, and a landscaped communal barbecue area can be found in the tent field; campfires are also permitted in the designated firepits (logs for sale onsite). Perhaps most importantly, though, is the Mad Apple Cider which is produced on the farm and is available to those staying at the site.

Unsurprisingly, the Quantock Hills are riddled with mountain bike trails and footpaths, one of which, the 'Coleridge Way', allows you to follow in the footsteps of STC, and is best appreciated after swatting up on a few poems beforehand. If you want to learn more you can also visit Coleridge Cottage, situated three miles from site. For many, though, the beaches are the main attraction. It's a scenic 40-minute walk to Kilve Beach, with a footpath leading directly from the campsite's edge (or a 5-minute drive). It's a great place to search for fossils as you dip in and out of the rock pools. Further east, the shingly beaches of Doniford and Warren Bay are similarly dotted with pockets of shiny water and are perfect for dog-walking and rockpooling – make sure you bring a net along!

WHO'S IN Glampers, campers, tents, caravans, motorhomes, campervans, well-behaved dogs – yes.

ON SITE 2 fields for tents, plus 3 hardstanding pitches, 30 seasonal pitches and 16 caravan pitches; 2 glamping pods also available. Washing-up facilities, laundry and toilet blocks with showers costing 50p for 5 minutes. Campfires are permitted at designated locations and there's a communal BBQ area. Games field adjacent to site.

OFF SITE The West Somerset Steam Train (01643 704996) can be boarded at Williton, a 10-minute walk away, and will take you to Minehead, stopping at restored stations along the way. Kilve Beach is a great place to visit in search of fossils and also has a number of rock pools. Visit nearby Fyne Court (01643 862452), an estate once owned by the Crosse family that was destroyed by a fire in 1894. Today visitors can take a tour of the beautiful gardens and learn about Fyne Court's most infamous resident, Andrew Crosse, known to the locals as the 'the thunder and lightning man'.

FOOD & DRINK Among other things, Moorhouse produces 'Mad Apple Cider', available to buy on site. The Plough (01278 741652) is a dog-friendly pub a 15-minute walk away, and The Hood Arms (01278 741210) in Kilve (also dog- and family-friendly) has a great beer garden and a play area for children, plus a large selection of local ales. The Chantry Tea Rooms (01278 741457) is a wonderful daytime option for cream teas and is located along the scenic walk to Kilve Beach.

GETTING THERE Travelling from Bridgwater on the A39, there is a brown tourist sign on your left for Moorhouse Campsite. At the sharp left-hand bend, turn right onto the road signed Lilstock and Stogursey; Moorhouse is the first entrance on your right.

OPEN March–November.

THE DAMAGE Pitch and 2 people £18–£22.50 per night. Additional person (3yrs+) £2.50. Pods (sleeping up to 4) £55–£60 per night.

middle stone farm

Middle Stone Farm, Brompton Ralph, Somerset TA4 2RT 01984 248443 www.middlestonefarm.com

You don't need to go on safari to stay in a safari tent these days; with alpacas, goats and rare-breed pigs and sheep, you can make a very British safari of your own at Middle Stone Farm. Binoculars aren't even required.

It seems fitting that Middle Stone Farm has named its three brand-new safari tents after birds of prey – Buzzard, Hawk and Kestrel. Positioned between Exmoor and the Quantock Hills, this remote patch of rural Somerset is an ideal sanctuary for wildlife. A resident barn owl hoots from the old barn opposite Catherine and Patrick's farmhouse and housemartins arrive beneath the eaves every summer, twigs in their beaks, ready to start building. Then there are the more catered-for critters: rare-breed pigs, sheep, chickens and alpacas grazing the meadow. All give the farm its unpretentious, backcountry atmosphere – that of an agricultural escape ideal for families. The safari tents are firmly at the upper end of the luxury scale, fully kitted out with everything you need, and housed beneath the forest green wingspan of their canvas roofs. The kitchen has cutlery, crockery and cooking utensils – best put to work on the artisan wood-burning oven – and there's even a small fridge located beneath the aptly named 'cupboard bed': a two-person cubbyhole in the wall that children particularly adore. Each safari tent has an en-suite shower room at the far end and a south-facing sun deck out front, plus a bubbling wood-fired hot tub you can relax in.

In its own private corner of the farm, a wooden glamping cabin offers an alternative to the three safari tents and can be booked on its own, or if you're quick, the tents and cabin can all be booked together to accommodate a larger group. The whitewashed deckhouse sleeps a family of four in a king-sized bed and separate bunkroom, while a large, open-plan living space has a slightly retro feel. It makes a nice contrast to the modern shower room and smart new wood-burning stove, adding its glowing warmth to the light and airy interior.

Evening campfires remind guests that, despite all the luxuries, this is still very much a camping holiday. You can purchase meat from the farm shop, too, if you want something to sear over the crackling flames. For a proper pint, it's a fair trek along the Somerset footpaths to the nearest local watering hole. But then, the real beauty of this campsite is its off-the-beaten track location while still being close to lots of appealing attractions. Hop into the car to get to the beaches of the Bristol Channel a few miles to the north, Exmoor National Park to the west, the Quantock Hills to the east or the market town of Taunton just south. Off the track it may be, but you needn't drive far for heaps of options.

Glamping only. Couples, families, large groups hiring whole site – yes. Tents, campervans and caravans – no.

ON SITE 3 safari tents and a holiday cabin. Tents sleep 6 each in a double room, twin room and a kitchen 'cupboard bed'. En-suite flushing loo, wood-fired shower and basin, plus every tent has its own hot tub. The kitchen has an electric fridge, gas cooker (outside), sink and a wood stove to cook on. Firepit and BBQs provided. Electricity for phone-charging (4G reception). Onsite shop selling local food and farm produce. Lots of animals (alpacas, sheep, pigs, chickens, goats and geese) and a playground with climbing frame, slide, swings, football net and toddler tractors. Kids can help feed the animals and, once a week in peak season, take a trailer ride around the field.

OFF SITE It's just 3 miles to Exmoor, home to some of the finest walking in the country, with Tarr Steps a particularly good target for families. A little further north, Kilve Beach is an Area of Special Scientific Interest and a top spot at which to go searching for fossils, while the sandy beach at Blue Anchor Bay is also popular – backed by The Smugglers Inn (01984 640385), serving excellent fish & chips.

FOOD & DRINK You can order lasagnes, chicken pies and ragus from the farm shop – convenient, since there aren't any pubs within walking distance. The nearest is the Notley Arms Inn on Exmoor (01984 656095) or, if you're heading east to the Quantock Hills, the excellent Rising Sun in West Bagborough (01823 432575) is 20 minutes' drive away.

GETTING THERE From Taunton, take the B3227 to Wiveliscombe, then the B3188 to Ford and up to Pitsford Hill. A ¼ of a mile from Pitsford Hill take the tiny lane on the left marked Brompton Ralph.

OPEN All year.

THE DAMAGE Safari tents from £550 for a 3-night weekend. Deckhouse holiday cabin from £140 for a 2-night stay.

kittisford barton

Kittisford Barton, Wellington, Somerset TA21 0RZ 01638 778325 www.lanternandlarks.co.uk

With cows, pigs and chickens to meet, you'd think a visit here would turn your children into wannabe farmers. But it's builders they become. Build a den in the woods. Build a dam in the stream. Build a pillow fort in the bedroom. Maybe bring a tool-kit along?

Nowhere typifies the British countryside quite like Kittisford Barton. On the western edge of Somerset, this newly opened glampsite sits within 260 acres of organic agricultural splendour. Fields fold into woodland and ponds pepper the landscape. Tiny streams trickle water towards the River Tone, surely the wiggliest waterway in the entire southwest, and mature, bushy hedgerows segment the fields into a patchwork of varied colour. If Somerset wants to lose its stereotype of farmers in their flat caps, this place isn't doing it any favours.

Yet the site is, in fact, strikingly modern. Not in an urban, gritty sense, but simply in terms of the luxuries on offer. Low-key, basic camping this is not. There are five safari tents in total, pitched in a large open field, giving both a sense of space and privacy. Each of the tents sleeps up to six people, with three separated bedrooms: a double room, a twin room and a children's room with bunk beds. On top of this, there's also a large open-plan living area with a dining space and a couple of sofas to relax on after a day exploring the surroundings. The kitchen offers real convenience, with gas hobs and all the cooking utensils you could need, while at the heart of it all is that one essential piece of glamping kit – a toasty wood-burning stove heating the entire tent with ease.

The location is certainly a boon for kids – think den-building in the woods and evening barbecues on the safari tent verandah – but don't be fooled by the rural atmosphere it maintains. While Kittisford Barton enjoys the peace and tranquillity that comes from being in the middle of the countryside, it is, in fact, only a 10-minute drive from junction 26 of the M5; a real convenience if you're a stickler for itineraries.

There's a Go Ape in nearby Haldon Forest so families can monkey their way across the treetops using zip wires and climbing nets, while the beaches of the north Somerset coast are just 35 minutes away by car. Exeter, meanwhile, is a speedy zip down the motorway – great for rainy days hiding in galleries and museums – while Exmoor, the closest of the lot, is the best when the sun's out, a staggering natural playground and one of the UK's quietest National Parks.

WHO'S IN Glamping only. Dogs, families, groups, couples – yes. Campervans, separate tents, motorhomes – no.

ON SITE 5 furnished safari tents, each sleeping up to 6 in 3 separate bedrooms. The tents have 1 double, 1 twin and a bunk bed with all bed linen provided. The safari tents are furnished with sofas, dining furniture, a wood-burning stove, a kitchen with gas hobs and cooking utensils and a bathroom with shower and toilet.

OFF SITE The UK's longest Heritage Railway, the West Somerset Railway (01643 704996), chugs all the way to the seaside town of Minehead. For walking and cycling, Exmoor National Park is nearest – grab an OS map and explore the vast moors – while the trails of the Blackdown Hills are on the doorstep. For something really different, Quad World (01392 881313) is a multi-award-winning quad-biking company with a large track that caters for everyone from first-timers to seasoned quad-bikers.

FOOD & DRINK Large and basic breakfast packs, a BBQ pack and a campfire pack can all be booked for cooking on the stove or campfire. 4 miles away, The Globe Inn (01823 400534) in Milverton is a great country pub with a lovely, family-friendly atmosphere and the 400-year-old Rock Inn (01984 623293; 3½ miles) in Watterow is now a top-quality gastro-pub with a nice, light interior and fantastic food.

GETTING THERE Leave the A38 directly opposite The Beambridge pub (near Wellington), signposted to Thorne St Margaret. Follow the signs to Thorne St Margaret, going straight across the next crossroads and taking the second right. Turn down the next left and go through the woods. At the end of this lane turn right. Stay on this road for 1½ miles, around a bend and over a bridge. After a hill, the site is on your right-hand side.

OPEN March–October.

THE DAMAGE Prices from £370 to £655 for a 3-night break.

hook farm

Gore Lane, Uplyme, Lyme Regis, Dorset DT7 3UU 01297 442801 www.hookfarm-uplyme.co.uk

The only thing that beats finding a fossil along this stretch of coastline is finding a campsite as good as this one. We've told you about it now, though. So finding a fossil better be next on your list.

Island-hopping dinosaurs were part of the scenery in these parts some 190 million years ago. Many lost their footing and fell into the sea, leaving their mark on what became known as the Jurassic Coast. Hunting down their fossils is a popular sport in the quaint harbour resort of Lyme Regis. Picturesque and peaceful, but within a stone's throw of the lively harbour town, Hook Farm offers the best of both rural and urban worlds. Tucked away in the small village of Uplyme, with views up the pretty Lym Valley, it's a lovely, leafy site that feels quite remote. Being in a designated Dark Valley, there's no light pollution at night, so just lie back and watch the stars emerge on a clear evening.

A few steps is all it takes to be warmly welcomed at reception, whisked past a section for caravans, and ushered into a beautiful terraced garden valley, where campers look like they're proudly privy to one of the best-kept camping secrets on the south coast.

The site is well-kept and welcoming, with pitches on several different levels, some spacious and open, others secluded and sheltered behind trees and bushes. Generous pitches allow space to spread out with gazebos and blankets. A dozen are tucked beside various bushy nooks and crannies, offering a little more privacy. You could select your patch according to your sleeping habits. Early risers should head west to enjoy the morning sun, and night owls looking for a lie-in can camp east, where the last rays of the day fall. Sunsets look best from the top of the hill, and the lower area is better shielded from the elements.

Friendly, quiet and gently undulating, it's a perfect place for families: children will enjoy the playground, complete with an old boat to clamber around in, while their parents will appreciate the well-stocked shop selling fresh bread and croissants in the mornings, and a village pub within easy strolling distance that serves local real ales and wholesome pub grub.

And if the peace and quiet of the countryside isn't enough, there's a great 45-minute walk down the valley of the River Lym into the cobbled backstreets and alleyways of Lyme Regis, with its bustling harbour, artsy gift shops, sandy beach and array of restaurants and cafés. You can either make it a round walk and return via the coastal path and the clifftop (the camp shop can provide details) or, if you can't face the steep walk back uphill, call a taxi, which will bring you back for about a fiver.

Fortunately for any young, eager fossil-hunters returning empty-handed from a day's beachcombing, plastic dinosaur eggs are sold in the campsite shop, which ought to lift spirits before the next outing.

WHO'S IN Tents, campervans, caravans, dogs (only certain breeds), groups by appointment – yes. Single-sex groups – no.

ON SITE 100 spacious pitches (58 with hook-ups), and 17 static caravans. Large, clean toilet blocks with solar-powered showers, freezers, a washing machine and dryer. Childrens' playground and a well-stocked shop selling local meat and eggs. No campfires, but off-ground BBQs okay.

OFF SITE There are great walks down the valley to Lyme Regis and along the coastal path, fossil-hunting beneath the local cliffs, and exploring the shops, cafés and restaurants of Lyme Regis. Lyme's Dinosaurland Fossil Museum (01297 443541) opens daily, plus you can do guided fossil walks along the coastline (07854 377519) – or, if the weather's good, you can just go to the beach.

FOOD & DRINK Hugh Fearnley-Whittingstall's River Cottage (01297 630302) is less than 2 miles away – book the tuktaxi to take you there and back. Or take your pick of the many places in Lyme Regis, from Thai on the seafront at Largigi (01297 442432) to high-end cuisine at Hix Oyster & Fish House (01297 446910) and the fantastically elaborate and delicious ice cream sundaes at Rinky Tinks on the prom.

GETTING THERE From Axminster head south on the A35, then right onto the B3165 (Lyme Road). In Uplyme, turn right opposite the Talbot Arms pub into Gore Lane; the campsite is on the right.

PUBLIC TRANSPORT Train to Axminster, Dorchester or Weymouth, then bus 31 to the Talbot Arms and up the steep hill to the site.

OPEN March–October half-term.

THE DAMAGE Tent plus 2 adults £10–£29 per night; children (5–16yrs) £2.50, under-5s free. Hook-up £3.50.

sea barn farm

Fleet, Weymouth, Dorset DT3 4ED 01305 782218 www.seabarnfarm.co.uk

There's not much you need to worry about when you pull up at Sea Barn Farm. The washblock facilities have all family eventualities covered and the stunning views from the campsite are sublime.

Tucked down single-track country roads, shaded with tall trees on either side, this little tenters' campsite is perfectly pitched atop Fleet Lagoon, Lyme Bay and the Jurassic Coast. Many of the pitches have countryside or sea views, and a low-key ambience thrives.

This is a traditional site with a well-stocked shop and facilities that include the two most impressive family bathrooms we've seen at any UK campsite, with a self-contained WC, shower, sink and even a bath. It is actually part of a larger operation that includes an adjacent campsite; guests can use their facilities too, which include an outdoor heated pool and a bar. So it's the best of both worlds – quiet camping, with extra entertainment just next door.

Regulars to Sea Barn tend to be visitors who travel from afar on long breaks. Parents like to pitch near the small children's playground. Older families enjoy all the grassy space for ball games. Climbers come to be near Portland's cliffs and quarries. And walkers just love the Fleet Lagoon – a unique nature reserve that attracts migrating waterfowl in spring and autumn. It's just a 500-metre stroll down private, scenic farm trails to the South West Coast Path, which runs along the shore of the lagoon. Take binoculars and a good bird book and you can tick the breeds off one by one.

WHO'S IN Tents, campervans, motorhomes, dogs (on leads) – yes. Groups – by arrangement. Caravans – no.

ON SITE Up to 250 pitches in peak summer, including 50 with hook-ups. 2 blocks with showers and toilets, 2 beautiful, large family shower rooms and disabled facilities. There's a laundry, bar and swimming pool at adjacent West Fleet Farm, a 15-minute walk away. No campfires.

OFF SITE You can walk from the site down to the Fleet Lagoon – a protected nature reserve – then follow the South West Coast Path along its length. Weymouth's bustling sands and Georgian promenade offer the quintessential seaside experience. Get up close to seals, seahorses and starfish at the Sea Life Centre (01202 666900) there or, for something really adventurous, treat yourself to a wreck dive at one of the many shipwrecks off the coast; dive boats can be chartered from Skin Deep Diving (01305 787372) in town.

FOOD & DRINK Some of Dorset's best seafood can be enjoyed at the famous Hive Café (01308 897070) while, slightly closer, The Elm Tree Inn (01305 871257) at Langton Herring specialises in game. The cattle grazing the surroundings produce amazing steaks; these are on the menu at the Bar in the Barn at West Fleet Campsite.

GETTING THERE Following the A354 from Dorchester to Weymouth, follow the signs for Bridport and the B3157. After Chickerell, turn left at the mini roundabout to Fleet. At the top of the hill, turn left at the crossroads.

OPEN March–October.

THE DAMAGE Pitch (plus 2 adults and a vehicle) £14–£27; childen (2–15yrs) £1–£3; under-2s free. Electrical hook-up pitch (plus 2 adults and a vehicle) £17–£30 per night.

eweleaze farm

Osmington, Dorset DT3 6ED 01305 833690 www.eweleaze.co.uk

A private beach on Dorset's Jurassic Coast is just for starters; locally-sourced organic produce is the main course, with marshmallows melted over a roaring campfire for pud. All digested with the help of stunning sea views. Yum!

Eweleaze is the Glastonbury Festival of UK campsites. Advance tickets sell out shortly after going on sale; resident cows are herded into other, temporary grassy accommodation; the production is super slick; and food and drink is available in abundance. The capacity is the largest in the UK, too; over a thousand people a day share this clifftop location. And like Glastonbury, its faithful fans return every year, won over by the curving Jurassic coastline and its own private, shingle beach. In daylight, it's quite a sight; at night, it's downright magical, lit up with campfires and twinkling fairy lights. Collect car passes at reception, stopping at the courtyard – home to a well-stocked shop, bakery, solar-powered showers, goats and puppies, geese and pigs – before searching for a spot. A 'no music policy', except on Saturdays, is the main difference between Eweleaze and Glastonbury. In fact, groups wishing to gas all night should head for the back fields where there is more privacy. The Beach field is closest to the beach and pontoon (a big hit with kids). The Track field is further from the sea and facilities, but you can keep your vehicle by your pitch. The Point field is quieter, but windy at night. You have to return again and again to find out what works best for you. But that, of course, is the whole point. And you will keep returning…

WHO'S IN Every man and his dog (camper, tent).

ON SITE Around 400 pitches over 8 fields; 33 showers; toilets in each field; firewood and hay bales available (for sitting and playing on); access to private beach with pontoon. Campfires allowed. Bakery, pizza and ice-cream huts. A shop (open 8am–9pm) sells food, drinks, gas, kites, camping and snorkelling gear, and charges mobiles (£1 per visit).

OFF SITE The South West Coast Path follows the coast in both directions from the campsite. Nearby Weymouth is a great spot for sailing; there are courses for adults and kids (£150–£165; 0845 3373214). If it rains, it's 5 miles to Dorchester, where there are heaps of museums.

FOOD & DRINK Try the bakery for morning goodies and wood-fired pizzas (midday–8pm). The onsite shop (open 8am–8pm) sells organic meats and local produce. The Smugglers Inn (01305 833125) in Osmington is a view-tastic 40-minute walk along the coast path. It has a pleasant family garden but is rammed in summer, so don't expect a quiet pint. For sunsets, head to The Cove House Inn (01305 820895).

GETTING THERE Take the A35 towards Dorchester then the B3390 and A353 to Osmington. After the village, turn left onto a dirt track to the farm. From the west on the A353, continue through Preston and, just before Osmington, turn right down the dirt track.

PUBLIC TRANSPORT The 503 bus from Weymouth stops at Waterside Holiday Park, a 300m walk away.

OPEN End July–end August.

THE DAMAGE Adults £8–£16 a night; children (3–14yrs) £4–£8 per night; under-3s free. Vehicles £10 (flat rate).

woodyhyde

Valley Road, Corfe Castle, Isle of Purbeck, Dorset BH20 5HT 01929 480274 www.woodyhyde.co.uk

Waving at steam trains and choosing which ice creams to eat have always been our favourite pastimes. Timeless, traditional Woodyhyde Campsite can offer both. Sometimes even at the same time.

Set among the iconic chalky downs of the Purbeck Hills, traditional, family-friendly Woodyhyde lies in Dorset's spiritual heart. The campsite is spread across three fields – a small one adjacent to the Swanage Steam Railway line, a spacious medium field (where you'll also find the main facilities block) and a large field with acres of room and broad, countryside views. Wide-open spaces here are just crying out for rowdy ball games or a few flicks of a frisbee. Kiddy bliss.

The leafy countryside vista is the perfect backdrop for some early morning yoga, but don't be alarmed if your meditation is interrupted with a sudden woosh and parp – that'll be the Swanage Steam Railway. The old engines whistle and wheeze past the site between Swanage and Corfe Castle. It's just a pity they don't stop right here; the nearest station is at Harman's Cross, 10-minutes' walk away. Being based on the Isle of Purbeck (in actual fact a peninsula, but we're not ones to quibble), you're just a stone's throw from some of the great beaches and coastal views of Dorset's famed Jurassic Coast. Be sure to take time to visit the huge natural limestone sea arch of Durdle Door.

With refreshingly understated facilities, acres of space to explore, steam trains and easy access to hidden coves, Woodyhyde is an utterly charming throwback to the camping of yesteryear. Sit back and relax as younger campers live out their own Blytonesque adventures.

WHO'S IN Tents, dogs, groups – yes. Caravans – no.

ON SITE Around 150 unmarked pitches on 3 fields, a handful with hook-ups. The large field is dog-free. A facilities block houses toilets, showers, disabled and family facilities and external washing-up sinks. A small shop at reception sells camping essentials and food basics. The site also offers ice-pack re-freezing and gas exchange.

OFF SITE The long, sandy Blue Flag beach at Studland Bay is just 10 minutes' drive away, and the entire Jurassic Coast, including Lulworth Cove and Durdle Door, is within easy reach. The ruins of Corfe Castle are in the nearby village of the same name, though cream teas in town may be even more popular. Hop on the steam train for a ride along the picturesque Swanage Steam Railway (01929 425800).

FOOD & DRINK Dorset cream teas are available everywhere, including the National Trust Tea Room in Corfe Castle. Alternatively, take a walk over Ballard Down, passing Old Harry Rocks, to the award-winning Bankes Arms Country Inn (01929 450225). It serves bar snacks, meals and a range of ales from local breweries.

GETTING THERE From the village of Corfe Castle, take the A351 towards Swanage. A mile outside Corfe, look out for the 'Woodyhyde' sign and turning on the right.

PUBLIC TRANSPORT Take the train to Wareham, then bus 142 to Harman's Cross. The bus will stop at the top of Valley Road and the campsite is about 350m down a track.

OPEN Start March–end October.

THE DAMAGE Adults £8, children (under 13) £4, a family of 4 £20, hook-up £5, shower tokens 50p.

botany camping

Bradley Road, Warminster, Wiltshire BA12 7JY 07713 404233 www.botanycamping.com

A rainbow spectrum of bell tents is on offer but green is the colour that stands out at Botany, with grassy space to run wild in and bushy hedgrows all around. And, with easy access to the UK's oldest safari park, you're all sorted for weekend activities.

The grand Elizabethan architecture of Longleat House vies for the public's attention with the exoticism and fun of the safari park behind. The first of its kind outside of Africa, the 500-species-strong park is kept slightly separate from the house, so those planning to admire the crystal-clad ballroom won't find monkeys on their bonnet, grasping at the windscreen wipers. On particularly still evenings, though, the roar of male lions can still be heard beyond the enclosure boundaries, carrying over the house to the surrounding Wiltshire countryside.

Beyond the range of the lions' roars and the chattering of howler monkeys lies a small campsite with a top location. Three miles from Longleat and ideally situated for exploring the rest of the county, Botany Camping is a charmingly simple site that also boasts a colourful cluster of bell tents for those looking for a more effortless stay. Choose this glamping option and you needn't bring much at all, other than your duvet and a devil-may-care attitude. Guests will find futon-style beds, eco-fuel heaters, cooking facilities, and all the utensils required, while campers and glampers alike still share the composting toilets and conventional flushing loos, along with four family shower rooms in a separate shelter.

Each pitch offers plenty of space and includes a firepit where campfires are not only allowed, but positively encouraged, with guests arriving to a thoughtful 'starter pack' including firelighters, wood, skewers and a hefty pack of marshmallows. The site also boasts a small shop at the entrance for buying essentials, while a supermarket in nearby Warminster is well placed for a larger shopping session.

The size of the campsite gives it a friendly, sociable atmosphere, but much of this is also down to the relaxed personality of Crispin, the ever-present yet unobtrusive manager, whose welcoming and helpful nature makes him a go-to man for queries of all kinds. It's no surprise, then, that such niceness has seen him charm his neighbours into offering 30 percent off Longleat tickets – very handy for family visitors.

Cycling, walking and fishing in the local countryside, along with Stonehenge, Bath and Salisbury (all 30 minutes away) makes Botany Camping a pleasant base for would-be explorers. And if you're there on a clear night you can even use the North Star to guide you; with a proper rural setting and no light pollution, this is the perfect place for admiring the night sky.

WHO'S IN Bell tent glampers, tent and campervan campers — yes. Caravans and pets — no.

ON SITE 6 camping pitches and 16 bell tents in 2 fields. More camping pitches available in August. Bell tents sleep up to 5 people and include a firepit, solar-powered fairy lights, a free campfire pack (wood, firelighters, marshmallows, skewers), a cool-box with frozen cool-blocks, beds, stoves, utensils and everything needed for cooking. You'll need to bring your own bedding and towels. Composting toilets and regular flushing loos plus 4 family shower rooms with sinks and hot water.

OFF SITE Longleat House and Safari Park (01985 844400) is less than 4 miles away — Crispin can get you 30% off your ticket price. Travel 30 minutes north to the historic city of Bath, or a similar distance in the opposite direction to Salisbury with its towering cathedral (01722 555120) and narrow streets. Be sure to stop at Stonehenge en route. Wardour Castle (01747 870487), Stourhead (01747 841152) and Wilton House (01722 746714) offer further local history.

FOOD & DRINK A small onsite shop sells essentials and sweet things for the kids, and there's a Morrisons in Warminster a mile away. There are also several pubs and restaurants in the town. The Snooty Fox (01985 846505) is one of the closest and best, serving good food in a friendly environment.

GETTING THERE As you come up the hill on Bradley Road, leaving Warminster, Botany Camping is the 2nd entrance on the left after the bridge.

PUBLIC TRANSPORT There is a railway station in Warminster. Botany Camping is also on national cycling route 24.

OPEN Mid February–September.

THE DAMAGE Camping £19–£24 per night (includes 2 people). Extra adults/children £10/£5. Bell tents £110–£130 per night.

camping games

Part of the reason why kids love to go camping so much is because it feels like one long party.

Away from all the techno intrusions into almost all areas of our lives, camping encourages a high degree of parent–child interaction. Put bluntly, you can't escape to the living room to read the Sunday papers, or to the office to check your emails and update your Facebook profile.

Chances are that you'll find yourself playing the sort of ridiculous, hilarious and occasionally humiliating games that you were always desperate for your parents to play with you when you were a child.

There's always plenty of room in every camping trip for the usual ball games, such as rounders or French cricket, so don't forget to fling bats, balls and rackets – and anything else that you think might be useful – into the boot of your car when packing. However, for wet weather (which is bound to happen), when you are confined under canvas, board games and playing cards are worth their weight in gold. But there's also something delightful about homemade games that are just plucked out of the ether.

What follows is a selection of some of our favourite games. They don't involve a single piece of kit, but they do involve a lot of fun.

letter chaos

Choose a single category, such as animals, girls' names, sweets or food. The first player calls out a single item from that category, and the next player has to use the last letter of that word to make the first letter of the next word. For example, if you choose animals, a round might go like this: horse, elephant, tiger, rhinoceros. You can make the game more complicated for older children, if you like, using more challenging categories, such as rivers or foreign cities. You might even find that you can trick a teenager into doing some geography revision without him or her even realising it! This is also a good game to play on long car journeys, particularly when you are driving to a far-flung campsite.

scavenger hunt

This is a brilliant game with which to while away an afternoon on the beach. Firstly, agree on a search area around your site, tent or beach-base. Then, devise a list of possible treasures that each child has to go and hunt for. For example, the list could include a bottle top, a feather, a piece of sea-smoothed glass, a completely round stone, and so on. Provide each child with a bucket (or an old yoghurt pot or similar container) to carry their treasures in and send them off to hunt for them, while you stretch out with a good book. For the game to last longer, make the items a bit harder to find, like a stone with a hole in it, a starfish or a crab's claw. The winner is the one who has collected the most treasures after an agreed period of time.

kick-the-can

Choose an open space, but ideally one with some natural hiding places. The best place is in a wood, or on sand dunes. One person is made 'king'/'queen', and must stand in the middle of the space beside the 'can'. This could be an old bucket or a stump of wood. The king/queen covers their face, counts to 25 and all the players must then hide. The aim is for the players to get close enough to the can to kick it. The king/queen must defend the can (now with eyes uncovered) and try to get a player out by tagging him. Once players are out they wait by the can in 'prison'. The other players then try to free the prisoners by kicking the can without being tagged. The game usually involves some high-speed chases to the can, and a lot of cheering.

wink murder

A good game for a wet afternoon, when you've visited every local castle there is and all anyone wants to do is sit in the tent. Rip up a sheet of paper into as many pieces as there are players. On one piece write the word 'murderer'. Fold the pieces and put them into a hat. Each person (sitting in a circle) takes a piece and checks whether they are the murderer, without letting anyone else see. The murderer then winks surreptitiously at each player, who will then 'die'. The murdered one counts to 10 before dying so that others can't guess who the murderer is. High drama and histrionics are fully permitted from the dying player at this point. The aim of the game is for the murderer to wink each player out without anyone guessing who the murderer is.

sports day

This works best with a large group of people, but even if you are in a small group it's still a lot of fun. If you want you can mark out a start and finish line with a line of flour, but you could just do it with things you have lying around on site, like a skipping rope, a spare guy rope or an anorak. Use your imagination when choosing the sort of heats that you want to have: fiercely competitive running races are a good place to start, but you could quickly graduate to the three-legged race, hopping race, running-backwards race, egg-and-spoon race and our favourite, the wheelbarrow race. You could race as teams or individually. Close your sports day with a grand presentation of prizes, maybe in the form of chocolates and sweets.

witch's ring

Mark out a small circle on the ground using flour or a rope (or mark the sand with a stick). Choose one player to be the 'witch'. She or he crouches in the circle while the other players walk around it. The witch then slowly rises and, on reaching full height, shouts 'Here I come!' She then dashes out and tries to catch another player. Anyone she catches is turned into something of her choice, for example a dog or a toad, and the player has to freeze in that pose. The whole thing is then repeated until all the players have been caught by the witch and she is surrounded by a field-full of strange-looking people contorted into silly shapes. Great fun and loads of hilarity!

harry's field

Abbotswell Road, Frogham, Fordingbridge, Hampshire SP6 2JA 074769 88855 www.newforestcampsite.com

Terry's Chocolate Orange, Gordon's Gin, Harry's Field... We're not sure who all these people are but we like what they do. And they all do exactly what they say on the tin. This really is just a field. But what an excellent field it is.

The New Forest may be 150 square miles in size, but its essential characteristics can be found in the immediate surroundings of Harry's Field. There's an appropriately named old English pub – The Foresters Arms – next door, footpaths leading immediately from the end of the lane, and wild ponies grazing in the heathland across the track. If you want to enjoy all the New Forest has to offer without spending your holiday in the car, Harry's Field is a great choice.

All the basics are here. The field is flat and well drained; there are showers, sinks and toilets at one end; and pitches are generously sized. There's also a great buzz about the place. The meadow affords room for up to 60 pitches, with two set aside for pre-pitched bell tents and, although they don't like big groups or late-night noise, the campsite still has a thoroughly sociable feel. Even the pub has something for everyone: while parents are tasting the local ales, kids can hang out with the donkeys who graze out front.

"We want to run Harry's Field as the sort of place we would love to camp ourselves", owner Vivien explains. The Sheriff family grew up on a staple of summer camping holidays and it's clear their approach to the site draws on classic camping memories: campfires are allowed, dogs are welcome, and annotated local maps are provided. If it's the sort of place they'd camp themselves, then we're happy to say that we'd certainly go camping with them.

WHO'S IN Tents, campervans and dogs – yes. Large groups and caravans – no.

ON SITE 60 grass pitches and 2 bell tents (one sleeping 4 the other 6; furnishings, beds and bedding provided). Toilets, showers, sheltered washing-up sinks, fridges and freezers. Campfires and BBQs allowed but must be off the grass. New Forest ponies and donkeys may try to join you in the field.

OFF SITE Walk, cycle or trot the local trails – Fir Tree Farm Riding Stables (01425 654744) is a short stroll away. For a secret discovery, stroll across the forest to find The Royal Oak pub (02380 812606) at Fritham – an excellent 1-hour walk or cycle ride with no roads or vehicles in sight.

FOOD & DRINK A small shop onsite sells local produce and the best pub in the area, serving excellent food – The Foresters Arms (01425 652294) – is right next door.

GETTING THERE Leave the M27 at junction 1 and take the 3rd exit on the roundabout (B3079). Go through Brook, following signs for Fordingbridge, and continue for 5 miles. Take the left fork onto the B3078 and follow this for 4 miles, past Sandy Balls Holiday Centre in Godshill, then take the 1st left (Blissford Road) for 2 miles, up onto Abbotswell Road. Go past Abbotswell car park and continue straight on. Harry's Field is on the right just before the Foresters Pub.

PUBLIC TRANSPORT The X3 bus runs between Salisbury and Bournemouth (both with train stations) stopping at Fordingbridge. Harry's Field is a 1½ mile walk from the bus stop on Southampton Road.

OPEN May bank holiday and throughout August.

THE DAMAGE From £27 per night for 2 people and a tent. 2-night minimum at the weekend, 3 nights on bank holidays.

red shoot camping park

Linwood, Near Ringwood, Hampshire BH24 3QT 01425 473789 www.redshoot-campingpark.com

Load the car, bring the bikes and take to the New Forest on two wheels. The rest of the time you can kick back and enjoy this spacious site – run by a family for families. The facilities are knock-out, and the campsite is a labour of love.

The best campsites for families are those that are run by families and there's no denying the credentials of Red Shoot Camping Park on that front. The same family has now been running the place for over half a century and bulbs and saplings planted when they first took over have now flourished into a green and well-laid-out camping space. The largely open, grassy meadow is peppered with magnificently mature trees along its edge, while the remaining gaps are bordered by a thick hedge offering shelter and natural greenery. It's simple yet appealing. All that family hard work has paid off.

The field itself has around 100 grass-only pitches, nearly half of which have electricity, resulting in a pleasant mix of campervans, caravans and a spread of family tents dotted here and there. While the general vibe is relaxed and traditional – with kids heading straight for the playground to let off post car-journey steam – the facilities are very much of the modern kind. There's underfloor heating throughout the toilet block, along with handy touches like hairdryers and a family shower room, while the reception shop defies its diminutive size with a stock of almost everything you could need.

The location, meanwhile, offers the best of both worlds. Within the New Forest, you can hop on a bike and camp without ever needing your car – perhaps the best way to get close to the flora and

fauna of the national park. Yet when you do buckle up again, there's not only the New Forest on your doorstep but also the beaches of Bournemouth and the south coast, allowing you to flit between seaside shenanigans and a weekend in the woods.

Perhaps the most convenient part of the location is the family-friendly pub that's on the doorstep. After a long day on the hoof you can nestle down in one of the pew-like wooden chairs in the Red Shoot Inn for a pint of Muddy Boot and recall all of the reasons you booked this campsite in the first place. Space: check. Facilities: check. Family-friendly: check. Things to do: check. A good local pub within walking distance: check and check. Probably all the same reasons that you'll come back again.

WHO'S IN Tents, campervans, caravans, motorhomes and dogs (on a lead at all times) – yes.

ON SITE 110 grass pitches, 46 with electrical hook-ups. Wash-blocks feature underfloor heating, plus showers, toilets, wash basins, hairdryers and shaver points, disabled facilities, a family shower room and chemical toilet disposal. Laundry room and local tourist info. Separate covered area for dish-washing. Ice-pack service available in the well-stocked shop and bakery. Outside there is a children's play area with a sandpit, balance beam and stepping stones for little ones, plus a rope climbing frame and activity castle for bigger kids. No campfires but BBQs okay.

OFF SITE Look out for the famous wild ponies and deer as you walk or cycle the local routes. If you struggle to spot them on your bike, though, try heading to the New Forest Safari in Burley or the deer-feeding station in Bolderwood – both a short drive away.

FOOD & DRINK An onsite shop sells essential groceries, freshly baked bread, homemade cakes, wine, beer and more. Adjacent to the camping field is the Red Shoot Inn (01425 475792), a traditional country pub that welcomes families, has live music on Sunday nights and hosts 3 annual beer festivals. Try the New Forest Gold or Tom Tipple from their in-house brewery. There are 2 other pubs within 3 miles of the site: the High Corner Inn (01425 473973) and the Alice Lisle (01425 474700). The nearest supermarket is a short drive away in Ringwood.

GETTING THERE From Ringwood take the A338 towards Fordingbridge/Salisbury. After 1½ miles, turn right down Ellingham Drove, then left at the T-junction, then first right signed to Linwood. Stay on this road for 1¾ miles until you see the Red Shoot Inn on the left. The camping park is behind the pub.

OPEN March–October.

THE DAMAGE Tent pitch including 2 people and car £18–£28 per night; electric hook-up £6.50 per night; children (3–15yrs) £4.50 per night; dogs £1.50 per night.

ninham country holidays

Ninham, Shanklin, Isle of Wight PO36 9PJ 01983 864243 www.ninham-holidays.co.uk

There's only one campsite you need to know about on the Isle of Wight when it comes to kid-friendly fun. With an outdoor pool, a well-equipped sports area and a perfect, safe location for exploring the island by bike, Ninham is top of the tree.

In the south-west of the aptly nicknamed 'garden isle', Ninham Country Holidays is a campsite with a secluded rural feel, yet one that remains a short distance from one of the island's nicest resorts. With its functional new town and quaint, thatched old town, Shanklin has been a popular part of the Isle of Wight since tourism here began. Where its cluster of houses merge into the woodland beyond, anyone with a good eye would spot the potential for a fantastic campsite or two, and Ninham is one of the Isle of Wight's best; a family-run camping park that is ideal for exploring the island.

Large but naturally broken up by trees and hedgerows, Ninham is a family-focused site based around the original farmhouse. The site's 220 pitches are divided across two separate fields, split by a wooded valley and surrounded by ageing trees that provide shelter and shade on warmer days. This secluded, countryside feel is accentuated by the long, private drive that takes campers down to the site, cutting them off from any road noise while also acting as a speedy cycle path back to the outside world.

Of the two fields, Orchard is the larger of the two with slightly more modern facilities (including an extremely handy family room with specialist showers and a baby bath); Willow Brook has its own separate facilities, which are more basic but functional and well-maintained. In both camping areas, pitches are kept mostly to the edges of the field, providing ample room in the centre and ensuring campers aren't crammed together. Those still wanting more from their pitch can even ask for the 'XL' option so motorhomes, awnings and cars can all easily be catered for.

Wander back to the main reception block and you'll find a welcoming indoor games room with a pool table, air hockey and more, along with free Wi-Fi and space to relax with a coffee or ice cream, served onsite. Outside, Ninham also boasts a sports area and outdoor heated swimming pool – ideal if the weather is a little too nippy to enjoy the sea at nearby Shanklin Beach.

The best way to explore the island is on two wheels. Surrounded by mature woodland and rolling countryside, there is a fabulous network of footpaths and cycle routes that lead directly from the campsite across Ninham Farm's sprawling 120 acres. Those who head south can link up with the famous Shanklin Chine, a twisting pathway with steps leading down into a mossy gorge, enlivened by the sound of a cascading waterfall. Meanwhile, by car, the rest of the island is open to you, its plethora of attractions and summer festivals providing an entertaining itinerary, whatever your taste.

WHO'S IN Tents, campervans, caravans, motorhomes, well-behaved dogs – yes. Groups – by prior arrangement only.

ON SITE 2 fields separated by a wooded valley. 140 pitches in 'Orchard' (no dogs during school holidays) and 80 pitches in 'Willow Brook', most with electric hook-ups. Separate facilities for each field – showers, toilets, basins and washing-up areas. Laundry facilities, games room, heated outdoor pool (without lifeguards) and a sports area with volleyball, badminton and table tennis.

OFF SITE Head into the seaside resort of Shanklin, with its thatched old town at the southern end overlooking the golden sands of the beach. The Shanklin Chine (01983 866432) is a popular attraction, a luscious green ravine with a walkway down the gorge-side to a handful of attractions at the bottom, including caged birds, chipmunks and a Victorian brine bath. Back at the top of the cliff, Rylstone Gardens are also a great place to escape the crowds.

FOOD & DRINK A coffee and ice-cream hut is open onsite during high season. There's a Morrisons supermarket 10 minutes' cycle (or a 5-minute drive) away and 2 farm shops: Farmer Jacks (01983 527530) in Arreton and The Garlic Farm (01983 865378) in Newchurch. In Shanklin, The Fisherman's Cottage (01983 863 882), hidden by the waterside, is an unpretentious thatched pub serving super-fresh fish.

GETTING THERE From the Cowes direction, go past the site entrance and proceed 400m to Morrisons supermarket roundabout, turn 180° and return to filter off left onto the site's drive. From the Ryde direction, take the A3055 and turn onto the A3056 at Lake. Continue for ½ mile, passing the Morrisons roundabout. The site is 400m further on the left.

PUBLIC TRANSPORT Shanklin train station is a 10-minute cycle away – linked directly to the mainland via Ryde Pier and the ferry to Portsmouth Harbour. The nearest bus stop is at the end of the campsite drive.

OPEN May–September.

THE DAMAGE A pitch (including 2 adults and electricity) £18.50–£25.75.

billycan camping

Manor Farm, Tortington, Arundel, West Sussex BN18 0BG 01903 882103 www.billycancamping.co.uk

Who can offer campfires beneath the starry skies? Who can offer a communal tent that looks like Aladdin's cave? Who can offer scrummy food hampers and unbeatable views? Billycan. And it's all waiting just for you.

If you're born in Arundel you're known as a mullet – not because you have a laughable hairdo but due to the presence of mullet in the River Arun, which cuts quietly through this West Sussex town. The river bestows Arundel with even more charm than it already has a right to, with its cobbled side streets, quaintly wilting timber and brick facades and the twin bookends of its cathedral and imposing castle.

You might want to start your visit at the castle: during the school holidays they frequently run events with little ones in mind, from jousting tournaments to living history days where folk in ancient attire regale you with tales from the past. Built in the late 11th century under the reign of William the Conqueror, the castle has been in the family of the Duke of Norfolk for over 800 years and its handsome, fairytale looks have seen it as a backdrop in everything from *Doctor Who* to *The Madness of King George*.

Equally regal for its stunning views of the castle town, and the majesty of its natural environment in a wild meadow, is Billycan Camping. If you're looking for style and comfort combined with an earthiness that takes you back to the days of your camping forays as a child, then you're in luck. In the words of its co-founder Alex: "We're family camping, not glamping, a place where kids can meet and like-minded adults get together around the communal campfire." But don't let her fool you entirely, for while the setting may be rustic, the style of its tipis, bell tents and other glamping options is beautifully eclectic. How many campsites have a communal safari tent that looks like a Bedouin palace – with fur throws on the floor, Moroccan lamps, and wicker chairs? Even the communal washing-up tent is photogenic. And we haven't even mentioned the interiors yet, whose bunting, shabby-chic throws, and bed linen have had newspaper travel editors waxing lyrical about this place.

The other founder, Sue, is a dab hand in the kitchen and alchemises homely stews to eat around the campfire on Friday evenings. She also prepares breakfast hampers bursting with pastries, jam, organic bacon and eggs – delivered to your tent on Saturday mornings.

Everything about Billycan, from the fairy-lit bridge to the beautiful view of the distant castle, is soothing and designed to get the city out of your system. This winter they're planting a wild meadow, so by the time you read this the air will be a-flicker with butterflies and the scent of flowers. Book ahead, though, as Billycan is unsurprisingly chock-a-block with outdoorsy Boden types and young wannabe pirates. Quite right too – it's one of the best glamping sites (sorry, campsites!) in Sussex.

WHO'S IN Glamping only. Tents, campervans, caravans – no. Groups, dogs (on a lead) – yes.

ON SITE 3 yurts (sleep 4–5), 5 bell tents (sleep 5) and a trio of 4-man scout tents spread around a 7-acre field, each one individually decked in shabby-chic style, bunting and cosy throws. Shower and loo cabin, and a communal tent done out like an Aladdin's cave. No electricity, so pathways are lit by tea lights. Look out for the pretty fairy-lit bridge into the adjoining field. Campfires in private firepits and there's also a communal fire. There's face-painting on Saturday mornings and art classes for the kids. And if that's not enough you can organise aromatherapy, an Indian head massage or reflexology to heal those weary feet, or a full-body Swedish massage. Treatments range in price from £20 for half an hour and £30 for an hour.

OFF SITE Bring bikes for getting around Arundel and exploring the river towpath. Children and adults alike will love the castle (01903 882173) for its events and activities, lavish interiors and beautiful gardens. There's Arundel Lido (01903 882404) for sweltering days, and nearby is Arundel Wetland Centre (01903 883355), where you can take a boat safari through the habitat of rare and endangered species. West Beach is walkable from the campsite, ideal for swimming and spotting lizards and oystercatchers. It's around 4 miles, so consider the age and patience of your children when you set off on the trek.

FOOD & DRINK Your hampers will keep you happy for breakfast, and there's a great communal BBQ too but, should you want a little more refinement, head into Arundel to Pappardelle (01903 882025) for freshly cooked Italian cuisine and home-made puddings. There's also a rather nice service worth mentioning to ale lovers – nearby Arundel Brewery can deliver its delicious brews to your tent!

GETTING THERE Head past Arundel on the A27 towards Chichester. At the first roundabout outside of town take the first left onto Ford Road; follow this for about a mile and you'll see Billycan on your right – look out for the white tents in the field through the hedge. It's easy to miss, so keep your eyes peeled. If you get to Arundel you've gone too far.

PUBLIC TRANSPORT Take a train to Arundel, from where it's easy to catch a cab to the site or walk the 15 minutes. Call the campsite for directions.

OPEN All year

THE DAMAGE Bell tents from £240 for a 2-night mid-week break. Yurts from £350 for a 2-night mid-week break. See website for further details.

blackberry wood

Streat Lane, Streat, Nr Ditchling, East Sussex BN6 8RS 01273 890 035 www.blackberrywood.com

The treehouse steals the headlines, but Blackberry Wood is really as diverse as the many trees that grow here. From pods, gypsy caravans and double-decker buses to the myriad of woodland and meadow tent pitches, there's something for everyone.

You can stay at Blackberry Wood any number of times but each visit is likely to feel completely different. This is partly because the secluded woodland changes with the seasons, but mainly because owner Tim is so focused on expanding his unique range of glamping accommodation that there's no anticipating what weird and wonderful structures you might find on your next visit. On our first encounter, a double-decker bus poked from a clearing and an assortment of revamped old caravans and bell tents were available for hire. Today, there are also the likes of an ex-RAF helicopter and a brand new treehouse with a shower room built inside its wonky turret!

It's the 'proper' camping, though, that's the real strength of this site. Nestled on the South Downs, the place is almost lost among the native woodland. Follow one of the footpaths leading into the rambling straggle of thicket to find 20 of the most coveted pitches, located in individual clearings with a firepit, some rudimentary seating and enough space for a medium-sized tent. Each spot feels gloriously secluded and, with so few pitches in this part of the site, there's a rare kind of peace among the trees, enhanced each evening by the soporific soundtrack of campfires gently fizzing. On the opposite side of the road, a second wooded camping area with a 'no kids and no groups' rule also does a roaring trade during

peak season, its popularity only waning as couples return to splash out on one of the glamping options instead. Indeed it's impossible to visit once and not return again to try out something new – the options just seem endless.

'Bubble' (a 1960s caravan) and a brightly painted gypsy wagon have a particular air of romance, while the red Routemaster bus, equipped with a kitchen/diner downstairs and a kids' soft-play area upstairs is on the more eccentric end of the spectrum. The full-sized RAF chopper with rotor blades still attached is an even more bizarre find. It's Tim's new treehouse, though, completed in 2016, that is perhaps his biggest pride and joy. Sleeping up to four adults (or two adults and three children) in a double bed and a snug loft bed, it features a well-equipped kitchen, a wood-burning stove and a sun terrace outside. Its higgledy-piggledy shape, formed by the naturally irregular branches, gives it a charming, storybook quality. It's a remarkably artistic design.

All these contraptions can be found scattered around the first small field when checking in at the reception caravan. Of course, reception was in a caravan at the time of writing, but we hear that NASA is selling off de-commissioned space shuttles so next year's check-in experience might be altogether quite different!

WHO'S IN Tents, glampers, dogs (on leads at all times) – yes. Motorhomes, caravans, groups – no.

ON SITE Tent pitches are each in their own private clearing, with a general family campsite on one side of the road and a quieter, adults-only site on the other. Glampers can choose from a helicopter, double-decker bus, 1960s caravan, gypsy wagon, wooden 'curvy cabin' and a treehouse (a second treehouse is already under construction for completion in late 2017). Campfires allowed in firepits; logs and BBQ coal available at reception, as well as basic food items. 4 hot showers (20p). Plenty of toilets and washing-up sinks.

OFF SITE The South Downs National Park is the newest in the UK, which means a lot of recent investment in the excellent paths and landscape. The site provides route maps for local walks and, depending on which direction you take, a 45-minute walk can take you to the village of Ditchling; the superb Jolly Sportsman pub (see below); or to the Black Cap viewpoint, a high point on the South Downs Way from where you can see all the way to the sea.

FOOD & DRINK The Jolly Sportsman (01273 890400) in East Chillington is fantastically snug and serves up a changing menu of gastropub specialities. Or visit the farmers' market on the second Friday of the month at Garden Pride Garden Centre (01273 846844) in Ditchling and cook up your own gastro delights.

GETTING THERE From the M23 continue south onto the A23 for 14 miles. Turn left onto the A273 for 1 mile, then bear right onto the B2112 (New Road) for 2 miles. Turn right onto the B2116 and turn left onto Streat Lane after 2 miles. You'll see the site signposted on the right.

PUBLIC TRANSPORT Trains run to Hassocks railway station from where a taxi will cost around £12. Or you can take the train to Plumpton station and make the 25-minute walk.

OPEN All year.

THE DAMAGE Camping from £10 (1 tent and 1 adult) per night. Glamping options from £40 (2 adults) per night. Extra adults £10, children (aged 3–15yrs) £5 per night.

WOWO

Wapsbourne Manor Farm, Sheffield Park, Nr Uckfield, East Sussex TN22 3QT 01825 723414 www.wowo.co.uk

With smoky campfires, old rope swings and lots of mud, this is not a site for the nanny-state obsessed. But go with the flow and this rural wonderland is the perfect outdoor adventure playground.

Wapsbourne Manor Farm, or 'Wowo', as it's affectionately known by a growing band of regulars, is a rare and beautiful thing – a great campsite within two hours' drive of London. No matter how many times you come back, this magical spot always seems to have something new to reveal: another field hidden behind the thicket, a secret pathway, a yurt nestled among the trees. And while the grass pitches in the camping fields come with plenty of surrounding space for game playing, there's a whole separate site that you might not see unless you go looking: the premium woodland camping pitches, otherwise known as the Tipi Trail. These eight pitches (christened with such delightfully spacey names as 'Hobbit', 'Woodland' and 'Little Owl') are secreted away in their own exclusive woodland setting and offer a fairy-tale setting for games of hide-and-seek. There's always something fun going on during summer weekend evenings too: soup suppers, pizza-making and plenty of mingling.

Children's entertainment is strictly of the old-school variety: climbing trees, swinging on tyres, rolling around in ditches, making camps in the undergrowth. In fact, the entire 150-acre site is a huge, natural adventure playground extending well beyond the four main camping areas. Saturday night is music night, with free camping for musicians in return for an 'open campfire'

policy allowing all-comers to join in around the fire. It's a hippified rule alright, but fitting for bohemian Wowo.

Nearby, the Bluebell Railway steam train is a big draw, as is Sheffield Park – arguably one of the country's finest gardens, sculpted in the late 1700s by the visionary landscape architect, Capability Brown. With the famous four lakes forming its centrepiece, the beds and borders exude vibrant explosions of colour at almost any time of the year. In autumn, black tupelos blend with the rusty reds of the maple and scarlet leaves of the oak. Spring brings a lively riot of daffodils and iconic Sussex bluebells. In summer there are flashy splodges of pink rhododendrons and the soft, magenta tones of azaleas, while in winter, with the grounds blanketed in snow, the gardens have an other-wordly quality. Cricket fans might also care to know that the park's pitch was the venue for the very first home tie between England and Australia in 1884.

But then, many weekend visitors don't get that far, happy to settle for the ample pleasures of exploring the grounds of Wowo for a few days. With the evening air scented with campfire smoke, the soft murmur of sociability and perhaps a musical soundtrack, this wonderful woodland hideaway just oozes back-to-basics appeal. Leave the rules at home. Let the kids roam free.

WHO'S IN Tents, campervans, dogs – yes. Caravans, motorhomes, large adult groups and groups of unsupervised under-18s – no.

ON SITE Grass camping pitches plus 8 'Tipi Trail' woodland pitches. 4 yurts, 3 luxury shepherd's huts and 2 vintage wagons. 2 bell tents in camping fields for hire during summer months with a covered cooking area. Wowo host a number of different workshops onsite, including bushcraft and foraging events, circus workshops, ukulele lessons, basketry and living willow courses. A woodland walk and Fairy Preservation Society workshop were introduced in 2016. Campfires are permitted (in firepits) and BBQs are permitted off the ground. There are 2 toilet blocks in the main reception/barn area as well as several lovely showers, including a large family shower block and an accessible shower room. In addition, every one of the camping fields contains at least 2 eco-flush toilets. A communal barn has a ping-pong table and a piano, free communal fridges and freezers, sofas, a play table and a coin-operated laundry. Wi-Fi is available across the campsite for a small charge. An onsite shop stocks a plethora of organic food goodies plus artisan bakery goods. A particularly nice touch at Wowo is the complimentary soup and freshly baked bread served on Saturday nights in the communal area, often with accompanying acoustic music. It's a great opportunity to meet other campers.

OFF SITE Go for a wander around the beautiful National Trust landscaped gardens at Sheffield Park (01825 790231), just up the road. Kids can run about, feed the swans and ducks by the lake and enjoy the children's trail. With a big collection of steam locomotives and a station right next door to Wowo, The Bluebell Railway (01825 720800) is perfect for a *Thomas the Tank Engine*-inspired day out. You can even travel to the campsite on board (see Public Transport). If it's sunny, why not nip down to Brighton for a day of good ol'-fashioned seaside frolicking?

FOOD & DRINK Wowo's reception sells home-produced eggs, veg, herbs and locally-sourced organic goodies, including ice cream. The Coach House tea room at Sheffield Park is open from 10am daily and serves hot meals from 12pm–2.30pm (call in to pick up some delicious organic cider, real ales and sparkling wines from the Vineyard Nursery tucked behind the walled garden). Head up the A275 to Trading Boundaries (01825 790200), a delightful café and eclectic furniture and antiques shop. There is also a great farm shop, the Dairy Shop, a bit further up the road on the left. There is no shortage of pubs in the area. The Sloop Inn (01444 831219) is a 30-minute walk from the campsite through shady woodland. There are also 3 decent pubs in Newick Village, which is an hour's walk along the River Ouse and through woodlands. Pre-booking is recommended for pub meals.

GETTING THERE From the M25, exit at junction 6 and take the A22, following the signs for the 'Bluebell Railway'. Keep going, past the railway on the right, and Wapsbourne Manor Farm is the second entrance on the right (look for big wooden signs). From the south, take the A275 north towards the Bluebell Railway/Sheffield Park. Once you've crossed over the A272 at Chailey, the campsite is a mile ahead on the left.

PUBLIC TRANSPORT The nearest regular station is Haywards Heath, from where a taxi costs about £15, but head to East Grinstead station instead and from there you can take the old-fashioned Bluebell Railway steam train all the way to Wowo, alighting at Sheffield Park station.

OPEN Tipi trail and glamping open all year round; camping from March–October.

THE DAMAGE Adults £10; children (4–16yrs) £5; under-4s free. Vehicles £5 per night. Firewood £6. One-off charge for dogs (£4.50). Tipi Trail pitches cost an extra £10 per night, except during winter. Glamping £124–£300. Musicians free by prior arrangement. There is a minimum stay of 2 nights.

embers camping bentley

Halland, Lewes, East Sussex BN8 5AF 0345 257 2267 www.emberscamping.co.uk

You don't need to be a classic car enthusiast to appreciate the Bentley Estate.
Along with the motor museum there's a miniature railway, a wildfowl reserve
and a stonking great campsite where campfires are practically obligatory.

Some 700 years ago, the pastoral parkland of
Bentley belonged to the Archbishop of Canterbury,
who later granted it to a local aristocrat. Perhaps
he sprinkled a little holy water among the
meadows because, when it comes to camping, this
place is truly blessed. On the first day the Lord
gaveth grassy fields and ageing oaks; on the second
he sculpted solid oak washrooms, a museum and
an adventure playground; and on the third day he
produced fire (and maybe a marshmallow or two).
The resulting Eden is a combination of simple
tent-only camping and a host of walkable activities
on the doorstep – a real camper's paradise,
surrounded by woodland and hedgerows, with
no electric hook-ups and just 45 ample pitches
despite its expansive grounds. Campfires, as you'll
guess from the site's name, are an essential part
of an evening beneath the stars here. And when
daylight returns, there's an endless list of things to
do. Head across the field to the Bentley Motor
Museum, where you can hop aboard the miniature
railway to tour the huge estate, or wander through
the wildfowl reserve, the most diverse private bird
collection in Europe.

After a relaxing coffee and bacon sarnie in
the campsite shop, hop in the car for a speedy
journey through the countryside (despite its rural
seclusion, some of the best attractions in Sussex
are just a short drive away). Embers Bentley is
both a gateway to the treasures of East Sussex

and a county jewel in its own right. The crooked
Georgian dwellings of Lewes are just a few miles
away, straddling the River Ouse as it carves
through the South Downs National Park. To the
east, the historic towns of Battle and Hastings
are preceded by Herstmonceux Castle. Then, of
course, there's the iconic chalk cliff coast, just a
25-minute drive away.

At Embers you get to blend quiet, authentic
camping with a collection of extra luxuries – the
wood-fired pizza oven, a popular little ice-cream
parlour and the option to hire 5-metre bell tents.
Throw in those nearby attractions and you've got
everything you need.

WHO'S IN Tent campers, groups – yes. Caravans, campervans, motorhomes, dogs – no.

ON SITE 45 spacious, tent-only pitches with no electrical hook-ups. A new, solid-oak wash-block containing 8 showers (4 male and 4 female), 3 loos for each sex, 2 urinals for the gents and 4 washing-up basins. The miniature railway, motor museum and adventure playground will keep the kids entertained, while the site is also host to an abundance of rare wildfowl. The Bentley Estate charge £8 per adult and £6 per child for day entry to these attractions. There are large spaces for games, pleasant local walks and a campsite shop.

OFF SITE Sussex is rich in history, with both Lewes Castle (01273 486290) and Herstmonceaux Castle (01323 833816) nearby. The famous sites of Battle (01424 775705) and Hastings lie just beyond. A 10-minute drive leads you to the South Downs National Park, stretching across the county and down to the Sussex Heritage Coast – home to good beaches and walks along the chalky cliffs.

FOOD & DRINK Onsite there is a shop selling milk, farm eggs, local meat and bacon, along with other camping essentials for the kids, such as ice cream, snacks and marshmallows. There is also an excellent wood-fired pizza oven. The nearest pubs are The Halfway House (01825 750382), The Laughing Fish (01825 750349) and The Anchor Inn (01273 400414), all within 1 or 2 miles of the site.

GETTING THERE The campsite is just off the A26, a few miles outside Lewes. Just follow the signs to the Bentley Wildfowl and Motor Museum where the campsite is located.

PUBLIC TRANSPORT London to Lewes or Uckfield by train, from where you can hop on bus 29/28, which takes you within a mile of the campsite, getting off at The Halfway House pub.

OPEN April–September, weekends and school holidays only.

THE DAMAGE From £17.50 per adult, £5 per child (4–16yrs), Under-4s free. Museum access not included (see On Site).

embers polesden lacey

Polesden Lacey Estate, Great Bookham, Nr Dorking, Surrey RH5 6BD 0345 257 2267 www.emberscamping.co.uk

Well, kings and queens have stayed here in their time, so surely you don't need any more of a recommendation than that? We can't confirm whether they slept in the grand Edwardian house or camped in the grounds, but the latter is good for us.

Within striking distance of London, in the heart of the Surrey Hills, National Trust-owned Polesden Lacey was originally one of the finest Regency houses in the UK. It was remodelled in Edwardian times and played host to King George VI and Queen Elizabeth on their honeymoon in the 1920s. Today you can camp here with access to the house, gardens and the rest of the estate, which – apart from the house itself, with its collection of paintings and furniture and mementoes of the many famous folk who passed through during the first half of the 20th century – has beautiful rose gardens and, most importantly, some 1400 acres of ancient woodlands and rolling farmland, explorable by way of multiple footpaths and bridleways.

As for the camping, there has been a site here since the 1960s, when it was used by the Girl Guides, but it has recently been transformed by the folk at Embers, an experienced group that has several, traditional campfire-friendly sites in the south-east. There are 35 grass pitches and a new oak-framed modern washroom, with underfloor heating, washbasins and piping-hot showers, plus a newly built wood-fired pizza oven by the campsite shop. It's a tent-only site, but you don't have to have your own tent to camp here: they hire out ready-pitched five-metre bell tents for families who are too posh to pitch, making it a popular spot for both camping and glamping devotees!

WHO'S IN Camping only. Tents – yes. Caravans, campervans, groups and dogs – no.

ON SITE 35 pitches, with a fire basket for each. Ready-pitched 5m bell tents (sleeping up to 6) also available. A newly built loo and shower block and a campsite shop selling food basics. The main onsite attraction is Polesdon Lacey itself; the house and grounds are free to campers during opening hours. The estate also hosts weekly evening events throughout the summer, from jazz evenings to bat walks.

OFF SITE Denbies Wine Estate (01306 876616; 4 miles) is the largest vineyard in the UK and offers tours and tastings for adults and activities for children, including horse and cart rides, birds of prey and storytelling events. Chessington World of Adventures (08716 634477; 10 miles), a short journey across the M25, is most popular with older children, though.

FOOD & DRINK The campsite shop sells drinks, snacks, ice creams and wood-fired pizzas in the evening, plus the nearby National Trust Granary and Cowshed Café serves tea, coffee, cakes and hot and cold food. Elsewhere, the Stepping Stones (01306 889932) in Westhumble, not far from the station, is a welcoming old pub with good food and a kids' menu.

GETTING THERE Leave the M25 at junction 9 and follow the A243 (signposted A24 Dorking) before picking up the A24 and then the A246 (following the brown signs). Don't miss the sign as you enter Great Bookham, indicating the left turn up to Polesden.

OPEN April–end September.

THE DAMAGE From £22.50 per adult, £7.50 per child (4–16yrs), under-4s free. Includes access to House and Gardens.

big hat bushcamp

Hardwick Lane, Lyne, Chertsey, Surrey KT16 0AF 07957 184341 www.bighatbushcamp.co.uk

This wonderful woodland wilderness is so close to London it almost beggars belief. Cook on open fires, build your own shelter and learn all the essential bushcraft tricks at this approachable wild camping site.

In these dizzyingly technological times, one can't help but feel we've all become... well... a little soft. Show a kid an iPad, they'll be yougoogling and myfacing before you can say 'angry-moshi-monster-birds'. But abandon them in deepest Alaskan wilderness and ask them to live off the land... (exasperated sigh). We jest, of course. But so reliant on gadgets and gizmos have our littl'uns become, we feel it's about time we got them reacquainted with making dens and getting their hands dirty. So if, like us, the only tweets you want to hear are strictly those of the avian kind, we think we've found the perfect spot. No long-haul flights required.

The brainchild of former British Army captain and all-round action man, Ian Brember, Big Hat Bushcamp invites you to 'go native' and learn traditional survival skills less than an hour from the capital. Big Hat's family-orientated woodland bushcraft courses take place on a secluded woodland spot in north Surrey, with an array of bespoke sessions (ranging from three hours to full weekends) that are both fun and educational. Campers of all ages are invited to invoke their inner Ray Mears, trying their hand at archery, orienteering, wilderness first-aid and much more. It's all done in a family-friendly, approachable way – ideal for children who want to be explorers but parents who want to stay comfortable and not end the day eating worms or drinking water out of mouldy old socks.

Most courses start with a period of jungle camp construction, which – along with learning how to build improvised shelters with ferns, branches and your own bare hands – is when guests put up their own hammocks and basha-shelters. It provides a surpringly great night's sleep after a busy day of activities. Or, if you prefer, you're welcome to bring your own tents along, or borrow one from the camp. Larger groups can also sleep in the main, wood-fire-heated safari tent at the centre of the site.

The setting lends itself to all sorts of activities – the thick ferny woods feel like a rather British jungle, belying the fact that you're less than a mile from the M25. A convenient outcome is that, when the outside world beckons, there's still historic Runnymede and Windsor just down the road and no shortage of places off site to visit. Yet when you want to stay hidden you can simply kick back among the trees and enjoy your newfound skillset. And when you're toasting your umpteenth marshmallow over the flickering flames and toying with your handmade commemorative survival bracelets, you'll be glad you heeded the call of the wild.

WHO'S IN Big Hat Bushcamp runs bushcraft courses (private and public, day and overnight) and is only available for 'just camping' on an exclusive hire basis. Groups are positively encouraged – for groups of 8+ an exclusive booking of the whole bushcamp is really good value.

ON SITE There are no set tent pitches and pitches cannot be booked like a regular campsite. Everything is 'jungle style' – a wooden outhouse houses the toilets and there are unlimited pitches in extensive woodland. Bushcraft courses include matchless fire-lighting, campfire cooking, archery, shelter and camp-building, wood-carving, night stealth games and more.

OFF SITE Historic Runnymede (01784 432891), location of the signing of the Magna Carta, is a great place for a picnic on its sunny willow-fringed riverbank. The hauntingly beautiful Air Force Memorial is also well worth a visit, not least for the expansive views over the capital. The Great Cockcrow Railway (01932 565474) is a cute miniature railway that has been in existence since 1946. For something more high-octane, Thorpe Park (0843 557 3627) and Legoland (0871 222 2001) are both within easy reach.

FOOD & DRINK It's all about the campfire cooking here. Ingredients and instruction are included in the course price. Try your hand at Dutch oven mac and cheese, griddle pancakes, stick bread and campfire pizza. For quality local produce, the Hardwick Lane Farm Shop (01932 564930) is just across the road, while The Kingfisher (01932 579811) in Chertsey serves up pub grub favourites.

GETTING THERE The site is 5 minutes from junction 11 of the M25 (between the M3 and A3). Directions given on booking.

PUBLIC TRANSPORT The site is 5 minutes from Chertsey station.

OPEN All year.

THE DAMAGE Private party rate: £30–£40 per person per day, £15–£25 per night, £6 per person per hour for half-day courses. Individual rate: £50 per person per day, £25 per person per night. Multi-child discounts available.

badgells wood camping

Badgell's Wood, Whitehorse Road, Meopham, Kent DA13 0UF 07528 609324 www.badgellswoodcamping.co.uk

Forget the car and leave a Hansel and Gretel trail into the trees to find the best pitches in this vast woodland site. Campfires, rope swings, old tracks and trenches make exploring every inch worthwhile.

It is almost a disservice to call Badgells Wood 'a campsite'. It feels more like you've driven into the woods, found a tranquil coppice clearing and slept the night hidden from the rest of the world. Such is the seclusion and simplicity of this back-to-nature spot that you forget it's really a carefully managed woodland, crafted so that every camper can have that authentic outdoors experience. In an ancient setting where campers play second fiddle to badgers, squirrels and chirping birdlife, Badgells Wood is a dreamy woodland escape.

Set in the 30-acre corner of a sprawling 250-acre forest, the campsite has ample space for pitches, each in their own unique spot and varying in size. Whether you want to tuck yourself away with a two-man tent, or park up a campervan with a group of friends, there'll be a pitch for you and, with peace and quiet at the top of this campsite's agenda, you can guarantee you won't be disturbed. Instead, kick back in your pocket of woodland paradise, kindle the campfire and let your kids loose among the trees.

With an interesting history as an old World War II training area, Badgells Wood is striped with concrete tracks and access is still easy by car. From the pitches themselves, pathways weave through the bluebell-clad floor to a sanitary block (which is built of wood, naturally) that houses sinks for washing-up and lovely hot showers. The ablutions offer some everyday luxury amid the wilderness, while compost loos are also dotted throughout the campsite for your convenience.

Though a hop in the car can take you to famous castles, pristine gardens and a host of family attractions, Badgells Wood Camping is a place to forget the modern world. In fact, you could easily forget the car altogether. On weekends, bushcraft courses are run by experienced outdoorsmen (and women) who tailor the course to all ages involved. Then the rest of the week can be spent refining your new skills, whittling around the campfire or building dens between the trees. Children will love the rope swings, hanging from sturdy oaks, or investigating the nature trail, while those in need of a stroll should take to one of the woods' many footpaths.

As the Badgells team rightfully proclaim, "if you prefer your campsite with mown lawns, plastic playgrounds and a swimming pool, then we're probably not for you". But those with a romantic yearning for an off-grid woodland escape should head straight for the Kent Downs. Badgells Wood Camping will certainly do the trick.

WHO'S IN Tents, campervans (limited number) and well-behaved dogs – yes. Young groups – no.

ON SITE Pitches consist of small clearings connected by footpaths. A well-constructed timber shelter houses washing-up sinks and showers, while compost loos are dotted across the site. A vast woodland to explore, rope swings to swing from and paths connecting to the North Downs Way and the Weald Way. Once a World War II training ground, old huts, tracks and a trench can still be glimpsed among the trees. Campfires permitted (in the pits provided) with grills and Dutch ovens for hire. Camping essentials sold in reception along with firewood and kindling. Foraging for firewood is not allowed.

OFF SITE If open space and country parks are your thing, stroll across the private parkland at the edge of the site to the top of the Kent Downs AONB for magnificent views. Walk a little further to Holly Hill or the café at Trosley Country Park (01303 815170). The megalithic Coldrum Stones (01732 810378) are also just a 20-minute walk from the site. Leeds Castle (01622 765400), Rochester Castle (08703 331181) and Hever Castle (01732 865224) are all less than a 45-minute drive.

FOOD & DRINK The nearest pubs are the Amazon and Tiger (01474 814705) in Harvel and The Green Man (01732 823575) in Hodsoll Street. Or head down to the Nevill Bull (01732 843193) in Birling. Those shopping for local produce should head for Harvel House Farm Shop (01474 814433) open on Friday and Saturday; their home-reared meat is perfect for the BBQ.

GETTING THERE The site is 2½ miles from the turning off the A227, between Meopham and Wrotham, near Vigo village. Turn onto Harvel Lane (signposted Vigo). Follow the road for 2 miles. Pass a left turn to Harvel, then a couple of houses and a yard; keep going for ½ mile. The entrance is on your right.

OPEN Easter–Halloween.

THE DAMAGE Adults £13–£17 per night; children (3yrs+) £6.50–£8 per night; under-3s free.

welsummer

Chalk House, Lenham Road, Kent ME17 1NQ 01622 843051 www.welsummercamping.com

A little site that's ideal for little campers. Even the owner used to pitch her tent in the woods here when she was a child. And with trees to climb, dens to build and eggs to collect, it's easy to see why.

If you're one of those people who lie awake at night fretting over whether you prefer camping in a field or in a wood (there's no shame in it, there are millions of us out there), you'll be relieved to learn that there is a select posse of sites that offers both, one of which is Welsummer.

On arrival, the site appears to be quite conventional: a short track off a minor road leads up to two small, flat camping fields. However, go through an unobtrusive gate underneath a beech tree and you enter a dense wood with half a dozen pitches that can only be described as naturalistic – the owners, Laura and Med, may have to point them out to you before you realise where they are. This is quite deliberate; Laura used to camp in these woods as a child and her aim is to offer others a taste of the joys she experienced back then. Situated on a smallholding with chickens roaming around a copse, bees zipping in and out of hives, and a miniature orchard containing native English apples, Welsummer is a laidback campsite that wears its quirky touches lightly (multi-coloured windsock, anyone?).

For those wanting more than a traditional grassy camping spot there is also a charming old Wendy house that the couple have converted into a cosy glamping den. With its proper bed, table and chairs, this tiny hut has everything you need to stay warm and dry. The green, wood finish allows the exterior to blend subtly into the surroundings, while the inside is small without being cramped. A cluster of bell tents means that any remaining glampers are catered for, too.

Prepare to make friends here. This is the sort of place where meals are shared with strangers, especially with those who make the schoolboy error of not lighting their fire early enough in the evening to cook their jacket potatoes by a reasonable hour so end up stuffing themselves with that delicacy of al fresco cooking: the half-incinerated marshmallow.

WHO'S IN Tents – yes. Campervans and caravans – no. Dogs by prior arrangement.

ON SITE Family-sized grassy pitches and smaller pitches in woodland. Pre-erected bell tents (sleeping up to 6) and a Wendy house (sleeping 2–3). Most pitches have a firepit (firewood £5). Male and female bathrooms each with 2 loos, 2 basins and 2 showers. Small shop selling basic foodstuffs, camping supplies, the smallholding's own free-range eggs, organically grown veg, hot drinks and homemade snacks (served all day). Kids will love the trees to climb and places to hide. Acoustic instruments and fireside singing positively encouraged, but radios and other electronica are frowned upon. No looting the woods for firewood.

OFF SITE Leeds Castle (01622 765400; 3¾ miles) is sheer stone-fortress perfection, and they run heaps of great activities for kids in summer. For something a bit different, visit Biddenden Vineyards for wine-tasting and 22 acres of vines to admire, with homemade juices for little ones.

FOOD & DRINK Walk the pleasant route to The King's Head (01622 850259) at Grafty Green, a 16th-century inn with tiled floor, oak-beamed ceilings and horse brasses on the walls.

GETTING THERE Exit the M20 at junction 8 and follow the A20. Turn right (from the west) or left (from the east) onto Chegworth Lane. At the junction, turn left onto the Lenham road; continue for 1¼ miles where you will find the double-gated entrance on the right just after a narrow section.

PUBLIC TRANSPORT Lenham or Harrietsham train stations are both 2 miles away but there's no bus service.

OPEN April–October.

THE DAMAGE Tent pitches: backpacker £15, small £20, family £30 per night. Bell tents £60–£90 per night (not including bedding and linen). Wendy house £70 per night.

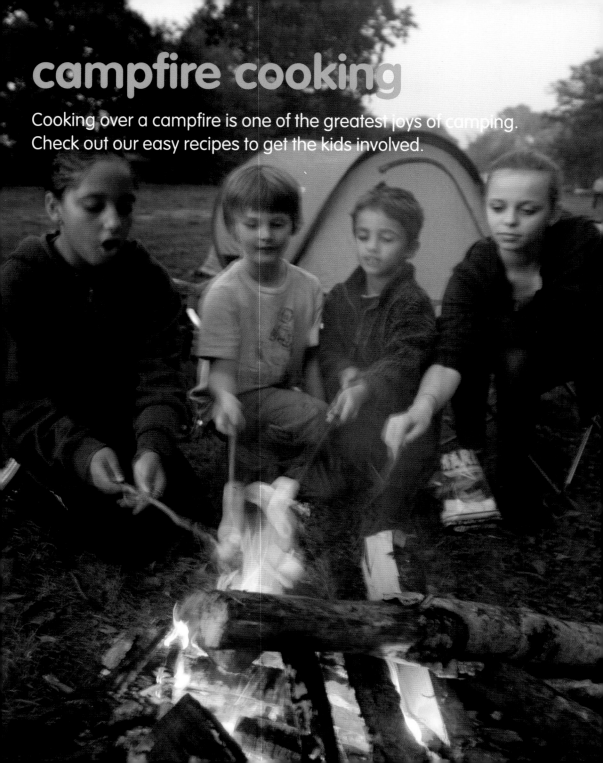

campfire cooking

Cooking over a campfire is one of the greatest joys of camping.
Check out our easy recipes to get the kids involved.

Campfire cooking with children is great, but it creates its own special challenges. You might have fond dreams of sourcing some locally caught fish to chef up with a bit of lemon and garlic, but it's quite likely that your children will be clamouring for good old burgers and marshmallows – again. If you're not careful you can spend an entire holiday eating Pringles for breakfast, Kit Kats for lunch and a portion of chips, if you're lucky, for supper.

Of course, that's also part of the fun of camping: it skewers domestic routine, which is precisely why children love it so very, very much.

What follows is by no means a definitive list of the kind of food you might want to cook with kids while camping (no, if you want that, then beg, borrow or steal a copy of the *Cool Camping Cookbook* for some proper tasty, grown-up-friendly fare).

Instead, the following recipes are guaranteed to bring great big smiles to your children's faces, even in the most inclement weather conditions. Forget all about the calories and the fact that you haven't clapped eyes on your toothbrush for the past week. That doesn't matter. Seeing your children having a great time is actually what it's all in aid of.

garlicky herb bread

Cream 150g of butter until it's nice and soft. Chop up a handful of fresh herbs. Parsley and chives are good choices, but at a push you could use tarragon or coriander instead. Add the herbs and two crushed cloves of garlic to the butter and mix it all together thoroughly. Add salt and pepper, too, if you like. Prepare thick slices of bread by toasting them on a grill over your fire or dry-frying them in a pan. When one side is toasted, spread with a generous knife-full of your butter mixture and return to the grill or pan so that the butter melts through.

orange eggs

Slice the top off an orange, setting the 'lid' to one side, then carefully scoop out the flesh while keeping the skin intact. If you have made any holes in the skin, plug them up with a bit of pith. Put a dab of butter inside each orange, and a pinch of salt and pepper, if you like. Carefully crack an egg into each orange, replace the 'lid', then wrap the whole thing in foil. Put the parcels onto some glowing coals in your fire. Allow them to cook for about 10–15 minutes before unwrapping them to eat. You can also use this method for other recipes – it's a real winner using a pre-bought muffin mix.

campfire baked apples

Cut the top off a large cooking apple then make an incision into its centre and remove as much core as you can – down to about halfway is fine. Mix a small handful of raisins with some brown sugar, cinnamon and nutmeg, if you have it. You can even chop up some pieces of ginger very finely or add a pinch of powdered ginger, but remember that younger children sometimes find fresh ginger a bit too hot. Put a blob of butter into the hole where the core was, then stuff the rest of it with the spicy raisin mix. Blackberries (or any berries you happen to have) can also work well as a stuffing. Put another blob of butter on the top, then wrap the stuffed apple in foil and cook on the fire for about 20 minutes.

chocolate banana treats

Carefully slice a banana open along one long side, leaving the two ends sealed. Break up some milk or plain chocolate (Dairy Milk works really well, as does flaked Flake and ripped Ripple). Make small incisions along the centre of the banana and wedge a bit of chocolate inside each incision. Push the remaining pieces of chocolate inside the skin of the banana, then wrap the whole lot in foil. Put the parcels onto the fire for 5–10 minutes, depending on the heat of your coals. When you unwrap your banana it should be soft and gooey, and the chocolate melted into a delicious mess.

frankfurter sausage rolls

Add a pinch of salt to 600g of self-raising flour and mix with enough water to form a basic dough. It shouldn't be too wet but, if it is, just add a bit more flour. Knead until smooth, then leave to chill out for a bit while you go and find some long, greenish sticks. Scrape the loose skin or bark from the sticks then spear thick Frankfurter sausages onto the end of each stick and push them three-quarters of the way down. Roll out sections of dough so that they are relatively thin, then wrap them carefully around your 'dogs'. Cook the rolls over some glowing coals. Don't try to cook over flames as the dogs will just burn. When the dough is cooked through your dogs should be sizzling, too. Slather with ketchup and mustard and eat immediately.

s'mores

For this British version of a classic American campfire treat, take two digestive biscuits and lay pieces of a favourite chocolate bar (Mars, Snickers, plain chocolate – anything goes – cut into slivers) on top of one. Toast a marshmallow (or two) to gooey perfection on the campfire or barbecue. Place the melted marshmallow(s) on top of the chocolate pieces, before squishing the second digestive biscuit on top to form a deliciously gooey sandwich. This is probably the best creation known to man, and kids absolutely love making as many as they can. Once you've done one, do s'more.

rushbanks farm

Bures Road, Wissington, Suffolk CO6 4NA   01245 790790   www.rushbanksfarm.co.uk

It's been around for over half a century but the things that make Rushbanks such a special campsite have been here longer still. The river, the views, the cute thatched villages and the pub just down the road... No wonder camping here never gets old.

Flatford Mill, famously pictured in John Constable's *The Hay Wain*, may be 15 miles away but you might well expect it to be closer when you come to Rushbanks Farm campsite, as the place has all the hallmarks of a Constable oil painting. The River Stour edges the grassland of the camping meadow, almost stationary it's so slow; fat lily pads pepper its edges and tall native trees tower on the opposite bank. There are no horses or carts, of course, and the odd campervan slightly modernises the scene. But the beauty of this campsite is that it's been left entirely untouched – a timeless slice of countryside where you can camp with minimal fuss. Opened in the 1950s and now run by the third generation of the Bates family, Rushbanks is the only campsite on the banks of the River Stour. Along with its location, it has some features that make it an easy choice for a *Cool Camping* recommendation. There's a thoroughly laidback atmosphere, campfires are permitted and the local pub is not only within walking distance but within paddling distance, too, with canoes available to rent for the scenic two-mile route.

For urban amenities it's a 20-minute drive into Colchester, but it's the rural charm of Dedham Vale that most appeals, from the 15th century buildings of nearby Nayland to moated, Tudor Kentwell Hall. It's difficult to imagine a more charming riverside campsite in the UK.

WHO'S IN Tents, campervans, groups, dogs (on a lead) – yes.
ON SITE Undesignated grass pitches. No electrical hook-ups. 2 riverside bell tents with a light, roll mats and firepit provided (bring bedding). Toilets, showers, a swing and play area, outdoor washing-up sink, water taps, chemical disposal and recycling. Free boat launch into the Stour. Rowing boat and canoe rental. Campfires permitted (pits for rent; logs for sale).
OFF SITE Rent a canoe and paddle to The Anchor at Nayland or take a stroll along the local footpaths – Wissington's Norman church is a short and pleasant walk away and it's 2 miles to Arger Fen Spouse's Vale Nature Reserve (01473 890089). John Constable's *The Hay Wain*, was painted at Flatford Mill in East Bergholt (01206 297110; 15 miles), now a popular attraction with occassional kid's activities in summer.
FOOD & DRINK The nearest pubs are The Anchor (01206 262313), a traditional riverside inn in Nayland, 1½ miles away, and The Lion (01206 263434), a similar distance away in Leavenheath. Slightly further afield, The Crown (01206 262001) in Stoke-by-Nayland is a particularly good gastropub.
GETTING THERE From Colchester, take the A134 to Nayland. At Nayland turn left, signposted 'Bures'. Follow the road for 1½ miles past a left-hand lane signed Wissington Church. Pass a group of cottages on the left and, shortly after a sign to the campsite, turn left through a gate and follow the farm track. From Bures, turn right by the church into Nayland Road. After 2¾ miles look for Rushbanks Farm on the left. Continue 100m and turn right through a gate. Follow the track to the waterside.
OPEN Mid April–start October.
THE DAMAGE £22 per tent (up to 2 adults and unlimited children). Extra adults £5 each. Bell tents £100 per night.

secret meadows

White House Farm Wildlife Site, Hasketon, Nr Woodbridge, Suffolk IP13 6JP 01394 382992 www.secretmeadows.co.uk

Family camping has never been so comfortable, nor so imaginative. Whether it's peeping from the oval window in the curvy Hobbit Box or steaming in the wood-fired hot tub, this is a place that will fuel creative little minds.

Suffolk is fast becoming something of the UK's glamping capital. The cluster of luxury glampsites scattered around England's eastern rump leave urban exiles spoiled for choice. And it isn't hard to see why. It's a rural, relatively unspoiled county, and very handy for the capital. But with such a wealth of posh pitches to choose from, it takes something pretty special to turn the head of blasé Londoners – in fact, something exactly like Secret Meadows.

Sadly 'secret' in all but name now (can you imagine having these meadows to yourself?!), Secret Meadows comprises six über-luxurious lodge-style tents spread across the idyllic 115-acre White House Farm. Each has a four-poster king-size bed, double cupboard bed and two singles, a fully equipped kitchen area, with fridge and barbecue, plus a loo and shower. The 'Gypsy's Rest' caravan and Middle-Earth themed 'Hobbit Box' are further options, tucked against brambly hedges and trees in the most secluded areas of the site. The former has been lovingly furnished in vintage style, adorned with cute little windows, a stable door, fitted cupboards and double bed (all hand-crafted). A neighbouring shepherd's hut provides extra living space, with a fully equipped kitchen, gas-powered refrigerator, wood-burning range cooker/stove, private loo and shower, hot running water, and a quirky built-in

double cupboard bed. The Hobbit Box, meanwhile, is precisely what it says on the tin – an old wooden horsebox with a large verandah on the back where a horse ramp used to be, while inside quirky oval windows and sumptuous furnishings give a modern edge to what still feels very much like fairytale-style accommodation. You don't have to be a Tolkien fan to appreciate its splendour.

We could, of course, go on – to tell you all about their Gold Green Tourism award, the bubbly wood-fired hot tub or the bespoke glamping packages on offer (which include bushcraft courses ranging from whittling your own knife to full-blown survival skills). There's certainly no doubt that Secret Meadows is an extremely slick operation. However, that doesn't really capture the spirit of the place. Secret Meadows oozes effortless rustic charm, and the site is also positively abuzz with wildlife; with everything from dragonflies to barn owls drawn to the vibrant wildflower meadows, it comes as no surprise to learn that you're actually staying within a designated 'County Wildlife Site'. With the Suffolk coast just waiting to be explored as well, and the charming town of Woodbridge nearby, Secret Meadows' location is also hard to beat. This is one secret that's well and truly out. Oh well...

WHO'S IN Glamping only. Tents, campervans, caravans, dogs – no. Groups – yes.

ON SITE 6 lodge tents (each sleeping 6), a gypsy caravan and accompanying hut (sleeping 4) and the Hobbit Box (sleeping 4). Tents feature a king-size 4-poster bed, special double enclosed wooden cabin bed and 2 singles (all bedding, linen and towels provided). All accommodation includes a fully equipped kitchen area with Belfast sink (hot and cold running water), slate worktop and a traditional kitchen dresser. There's a gas-powered fridge, BBQ, dining area with candle chandelier and a comfy sofa. Each unit has its own private loo and shower.

OFF SITE Nearby Woodbridge is a nice town and the Suffolk Coast is a short drive away, with Orford and cosmopolitan Aldeburgh both well worth exploring. Just outside Woodbridge, the important Anglo-Saxon burial mounds of Sutton Hoo (01394 389700) are essential visiting for any budding little Tony Robinsons.

FOOD & DRINK There's an onsite farm shop stocking a wide range of locally sourced delectables, breakfast hampers and BBQ boxes. For food, the excellent, redbrick Turks Head (01394 610 343) is within easy walking distance, while The Galley (01394 380055) in nearby Woodbridge offers a refined à la carte menu.

GETTING THERE Leave the A12 just north of Woodbridge, following signs to Bredfield. Follow the road for ¾ mile, then take the first left, signed to Hasketon. Follow this road for exactly 1 mile, then take a right turn (opposite some houses). The site is ½ mile along this road on the right.

PUBLIC TRANSPORT Woodbridge is the nearest train station. The regular 64 bus runs from there to Hasketon Church.

OPEN March–November.

THE DAMAGE Lodge tents from £545 for a 3-night weekend stay, from £369 for a 4-night midweek stay, from £981 for a week's stay. Gypsy's Rest and the Hobbit Box from £445 for a 3-night weekend stay, from £357 for a 4-night midweek stay, and from £779 for a week's stay.

happy days retro vacations

Wardspring Farm, Leiston Road, Saxmundham, Suffolk IP17 1TG 01728 603424 www.happydaysrv.co.uk

Retro Airstreams and vintage camping trailers take parents back to their youth, while an old army truck and playground keep children occupied as well. Happy families, happy camping, Happy Days.

Moving out of London and living 'the dream' usually remains just that – a dream – for most of us. But for Kevin Armstrong, turning 40 and enduring a nasty motorbike accident turned the typical midlife crisis of 'fancy cars, fancy hairpieces and fast woman' into something more creative. His wife, Jenni, had fallen in love with beautiful, vintage Airstream caravans and so, on moving back to her childhood haunt, the couple threw themselves into the business of seeking out and then doing up their own.

Formerly based in East Dorset, the Happy Days team relocated to the tranquil outskirts of the peaceful Suffolk market town of Saxmundham in 2015. Their newly acquired spot features ample room for their eight signature trailers and space for an additional two tents or retro caravans/campers. Plans are also afoot for an eighth American addition to the group, Wanda the Streamline trailer.

The current four and five-berth Airstreams are each decorated in various themes (Betsy – red; Gloria – burgundy and strawberry; Peggy – blue; Annie – flamingoes; Dee Dee – floral and gingham; Elsie – green vintage; and Netty – 70s

retro) and feature original wood veneer interiors. Every attention to detail has been poured into the furnishings, with crochet blankets, quaint curtains and kitsch cushions, while the retro vibe of small items like the radio or strings of fairy lights and bunting add to the authentic feel of it all. Outside, meanwhile, the new space has given room for adding a little extra flair to the proceedings. A polytunnel has been ingeniously converted into a cool social space – an all-season option for escaping the worst of the British weather – and a fantastic kids play area with swings, slide and a giant trampoline has been crafted around the site's magnificently playful centrepiece: a 1950s French army truck that even the grown-ups will be clambering into.

The result is a site that really does seem to reflect Kevin and Jenni's dreams. Cooking up a feast on the gas cooker and eating it al fresco on the picnic table, you can't help but envy them and their little pocket of glamping paradise. And as the fairy lights twinkle and the sun's light creates a farewell dance over the hedgerows opposite, it really is Happy Days indeed.

WHO'S IN Retro glamping and camping only. Family groups – yes. Dogs (on a lead) permitted in 2 of the Airstreams. No all-adult groups during school holidays or bank holidays.

ON SITE 8 Airstreams, each with its own colour scheme, and 2 additional camping pitches for visiting vintage caravans, campervans or retro tents. Each airstream has a firepit (wood available £5), fridge/freezer, kettle, cooker, sink, toaster, radio, DVD player, table and chairs, cooking utensils, WC for night-time use, games, torches, blanket plus other essential items including washing-up liquid, tea, coffee, salt and pepper. Wash-block features individual shower rooms and space for a family. Separate disabled facilities.

OFF SITE You're very well located for best of the Suffolk Coast, with the seaside-shingle splendour of well-heeled Aldeburgh and neighbouring Thorpeness close at hand, along with historic Dunwich and the fabulous Minsmere RSPB Reserve (01728 648218) a little further north. Beyond that, Walberswick and Southwold also beckon – the latter has a fine old pier and a great beach and is the long-established home of Adnam's Brewery, which runs regular tours. Finally, the Long Shop Museum in workaday Leiston is definitely worth a visit (01728 832189); a pioneer of steam-driven equipment that used to be the town's main employer before the nearby Sizewell nuclear power stations came along.

FOOD & DRINK The Bell at Sax (01728 602331) is a fantastic restaurant mere minutes away, helmed by Terence Conran's former executive chef. Expect a menu of delicious, locally sourced dishes at reasonable prices, albeit with little concessions to kids so parents with very little children should try elsewhere. The Dolphin Inn (01728 454994) at Thorpeness is a welcoming Suffolk country pub, with a log fire, a choice of local brews and a menu of hearty yet sophisticated favourites such as oven-baked chicken breast, smoked bacon and onion hash, green beans and crispy fried egg. In Aldeburgh, The Lighthouse (01728 453377) is a great, informal restaurant that's very popular and always busy, while in Southwold you could try the food on offer at the excellent Lord Nelson pub (01502 722079). In Walberswick try The Anchor, which is a cool and long-established gastropub with a good selection of real ales (01502 722122).

GETTING THERE Take the B1119 Leiston Road from the centre of Saxmundham, between Tesco and Waitrose, following it out of town for 1 mile. On your left you will see a small copse of trees, and immediately after that a wind turbine and a line of trees as the road curves. Take the left turn up the track and you have arrived.

OPEN Mid March–end October.

THE DAMAGE From £240 for a 3-night weekend in an Airstream (Fri–Mon) stay. Up to £720 for a week in high season. Whole site hire available.

swattesfield

Gislingham Road, Thornham Magna, Suffolk IP23 8HH 01379 788558 www.swattesfieldcampsite.co.uk

Bring bikes or good walking shoes to wear the kids out or head to the playground on the local village green. Then enjoy the wildlife and the peace and quiet of this smallsville rural campsite run by a father-and-son team.

Deep in the wilds of north Suffolk, keen camper Jonathan set up this seven-acre campsite with his dad in 2011. It's a simple spot exuding a *Cool Camping* vibe, with two grassy fields separated by a small lake with some adjoining woodland to explore. The position is perfect for bucolic strolls across the well-marked paths and bridleways of nearby Thornham Walks and for exploring the historic Walled Garden on the adjacent Thornham Estate, which has recently been restored and is open on weekends.

Above all, however, it's a great place to simply do nothing and enjoy getting back to nature. You can erect your tent in the bottom field, whih is spacious, green and peppered with daisies in the summer, or pitch up in the woodland beyond – ideal for those seeking a little more privacy. Glampers meanwhile have a range of options. Initially, Swattesfield kicked things off by offering boutique bell tents, complete with a full-size double bed and handy cooking facilities. Buoyed by their success, they then went on to build further glamping structures. Guests can now also find a pair of octagonal timber huts with cute, peek-a-boo windows, and a converted Suffolk hay cart, refurbished to provide comfort, warmth and style while retaining its historic charm.

All of the glamping units come with their own gas ring, cooking utensils, picnic bench and campfire-pit, with firewood available onsite.

Regular tent campers, meanwhile, are equally encouraged to keep things old-school, with firepits for use and marshmallows for sale. It's all part of the character of the place – a character that can only be realised by an owner who clearly loves camping himself. Some of Jonathan's mates even built him a fabulous outdoor pizza oven almost entirely out of recycled materials – definitely something to use at some point during your stay!

Overall, Swattesfield is a site with a pleasantly chilled-out atmosphere situated in a very special location. The space the meadow affords could easily have been a recipe for 'Tetris tents' in their dozens, yet instead the opposite has been created. And for that we couldn't be more grateful.

WHO'S IN Tents, small campervans, dogs – yes. Caravans, big groups, young groups – no.

ON SITE 15 grass pitches, 3 bell tents (sleeping 4/5), 2 pixie huts (sleeping 2 adults and 2 children) and a converted Suffolk hay cart (sleeping 2 adults and 2 children). Campfires allowed in the pits provided and homemade pizza oven for use. Simple but clean toilet block, with 2 showers, 6 sinks and 6 toilets, plus outdoor washing-up area. A small shop sells camping equipment and food essentials and you can re-freeze ice packs there. Library for use and board games to borrow.

OFF SITE 'Thornham Walks' is directly accessible from the site – 12 miles of waymarked footpaths (open daily 9am–6pm, April–Oct; shorter hours outside this period). It's a 15-minute walk to Gislingham, where there's a village shop and a play area on the green for little ones. By car, the Museum of East Anglian Life (01449 612229) is 20 minutes away and has plenty for everyone, including steam engines, a farm zoo, gypsy caravans and events throughout the year.

FOOD & DRINK The Thornham Estate's Forge Tea Room (01379 783035) and Thornham Coach House (01379 783373) are a 15–20-minute walk away and serve lunch and dinner. Or try the Four Horseshoes pub (01379 678777) in nearby Thornham Magna, a 25-minute walk away.

GETTING THERE From the A140, follow the signs to Thornham Walks and continue past the entrance and along Gislingham Road for about a mile. Turn right after the school sign and a Swattesfield Campsite sign on a tree marks the entrance. Coming from the opposite direction, through Gislingham, exit the village past the church and head towards Thornham Magna; ½ mile after the village you will see the school sign and the campsite sign.

OPEN March–end September.

THE DAMAGE Pitches from £17 per night. Pixie huts from £190 for a Mon–Fri or Fri–Mon break. Bell tents from £175 for the same. Hay Cart from £190 for the same periods.

ling's meadow

Stanton Road Farm, North Common, Hepworth, Diss, Norfolk IP22 2PR   01359 250594 lingsmeadow. co.uk

Children chase one another through the long, wild grass like a savannah scene in the latest David Attenborough documentary. But there are luxuries and extra comforts too, craftily woven into this overwhelmingly natural site.

A butterfly dances delicately over the lush grass swaying lazily in the soothing midsummer breeze. Buzzards and kestrels circle overhead, spying on hares that dot the meadow below. And, amid this idyllic scene, you are reclining in the sun, the laughter of children embarking on an adventure in the background. Sounds like a certain popular cider brand's latest cheesy advert, right? Wrong. For this idyllic scene is what awaits those campers lucky enough to stumble upon Ling's Meadow.

Nestled within a particularly peaceful pocket of their 80-acre wheat and barley farm, close to the Suffolk border, Ling's Meadow is the Shearer family's camping dream come true. In a four-acre meadow, this seamless new glamping venture merges effortlessly into its surroundings. The beautiful blue living van has been built by a local carpenter, with exquisite beds carved from knobbly natural wood, while the gypsy wagon and shepherd's hut (booked together and sleeping four) were found, delapidated on nearby farms and painstakingly restored to their gorgeous current standard. There are also twin five-metre bell tents, fully furnished and bedecked. The roll-up sides simply beckoning you in to unwind.

For regular campers, spacious, circular tent pitches have been hued into the meadow grass with meandering, mown paths connecting them. It leaves a natural network to explore. In the height of summer when the grass is at its tallest, the pitches offer the perfect secluded hideaway.

So as not to compromise the tranquillity of this bucolic bolthole, only 25 guests can be accommodated at any one time. The verdant meadow is also refreshingly vehicle-free, with trolleys provided for lugging your gear around. No man (or woman) is an island, though, and for those looking to shoot the breeze with their fellow camping *compadres*, the communal kitchen and dining area is the perfect arena for socialising.

Offsite, East Anglia is yours to explore, from the Broads and the coast to charming rural villages and their medieval churches. In keeping with the site's green ethos (water is recycled, so it can be used on the farm garden), guests are encouraged to explore the region on two wheels and, helpfully National Cycle Network Route 13 and Regional Route 30 run just to the north of the site.

At its heart, Ling's Meadow is a campsite run by people who genuinely adore camping and who know exactly what campers want. As friendly matriarch Kath says, "We love camping in our own bell tent and are happy to admit that occasionally we enjoy a bit of luxury too. Because we enjoy it so much our aim is to provide an affordable glamping experience." Many campsites try to bridge that gap between rustic and luxury, with varying degrees of success. With their boundless hospitality, dished out from their gorgeous 17th-century farmhouse, we think the Shearers have it pretty spot-on.

WHO'S IN Glampers, campers, small groups – yes. Caravans, campervans, dogs – no. Larger groups are welcome to book the entire site (up to 20 people).

ON SITE 6 grass camping pitches, 2 fully furnished bell tents (sleeping up to 5 in 1 double bed and 2 futons plus an inflatable mattress); 1 fully furnished living van (sleeping up to 4 in 2 double bunks); 1 restored shepherd's hut and 1 restored gypsy caravan (booked together; sleeping up to 4 in 2 double beds); 2 pre-pitched 4–5 person unfurnished bell tents also available to hire. Linen and towels provided for 7-night glamping stay. Extra mattress, travel cot, and blankets available. Bell tents, living van and shepherd's hut include firepits and grills, with a complimentary basket of logs provided (wood can also be bought on site) and outdoor seating. Stoves and all cooking utensils provided, plus cool-boxes with freezer-blocks and water carriers. There are 2 composting toilets and 1 wood-heated shower. For other campers there is a communal kitchen tent with cooking equipment, dining area and washing-up facilities. Secure cycle shed with bike tools and cycle route information available. Bikes to borrow (limited supply – book in advance). Bike hose-down area and kit-washing available. Firepits to borrow for campfires.

OFF SITE The site is ideally located to explore the best of East Anglia, with Bury St Edmunds, Norwich, Cambridge and the North Norfolk Coast and Broads all within easy reach. The Peddars Way Walk is one of the area's best walking trails, while High Lodge Thetford Forest is a great place to head for if you want to explore on two wheels. Local pick-up by the campsite owners is available for walkers/guests using public transport. For a day at the seaside, Holkham Bay and Southwold's famous pier and lighthouse are two options. Kids and parents alike will love Jimmy's Farm (01473 604206) just outside Ipswich and the award-winning treehouse adventure park, BeWILDerwood (01692 633033), just outside the pretty riverside village of Horning in the heart of the Broads.

FOOD & DRINK The Mill Inn (01359 221018) is just a 3-mile walk from the site in nearby Market Weston – perfect for a sample of the local ales and pub grub. For ale aficionados, the Old Chimneys Brewery (01359 221411) and shop is also nearby, as is St George's Whisky Distillery (01953 717939), which offers tours as well as the chance to buy. Wyken Vineyards (01359 250262) is just a short cycle ride away – it is also home to the gorgeous, oak-beamed Leaping Hare (01359 250287) restaurant and a country store. For the finest local produce, Wyken also holds a farmer's market every Saturday. Further afield, The Bell Inn (01379 898445) at Rickinghall and No 4 Hatter Street (01284 754477) are decent shouts for food. Kath can also provide food hampers brimming with local produce – enquire before booking.

GETTING THERE Ling's Meadow is just off the B111 between Barningham and Stanton. From further afield you can reach the B111 via the A14 and then the A143. The A14 links up with the A11 and M11 from the west, the A1 from the north and the A12 from the south-east.

PUBLIC TRANSPORT The nearest railway stations are Thetford, Diss and Stowmarket. Bury St Edmunds is only slightly further away. All have taxi ranks and good bus links. Reasonably regular buses run from Diss and Bury St Edmunds to Hepworth. Both take about half an hour.

OPEN May–end September

THE DAMAGE Camping £7–£10 per person per night, children (3–5yrs) £3.50–£5 per night, under-3s free; add £15 per night for a basic, pre-pitched bell tent. Furnished bell tents £60–£80 per night; living van/shepherd's hut and gypsy caravan £68–£90 per night – 2-night minimum (3 on bank holidays). Cyclists, walkers and those using public transport also receive a 10% discount.

wardley hill campsite

Wardley Hill Road, Kirby Cane, The Waveney Valley, Norfolk NR35 2PQ 07733 306543 www.wardleyhillcampsite.com

Hunting for bugs in the streams and den-building in the woods entertains little tots on site, while there's a play park within walking distance and safe sea swimming a short drive away.

The meandering Waveney River carves the border between Norfolk and Suffolk, its glistening waters drifting eastward into the Broads. The wide green flood plains, dotted with pockets of woodland, are home not only to handsome market towns that have stood for centuries, but also to a plethora of wildlife with a far longer-reaching history. It is here, among the birds and the bees, the bushes and the trees, that Wardley Hill Campsite can be found. A simple rural meadow in the beautiful Waveney valley.

Wardley Hill is actually a relatively new site, opened back in 2014 by owners Joe and Holly Putman. The lush, six-acre space is a seemingly unmanaged mix of long wild grass, ageing oaks and trickling streams, though in fact the field has been carefully developed in subtle, ecologically friendly ways. Among the meadows, wild flower seeds have been scattered, boosting the butterfly numbers, while wider areas of mown grass still provide practical camping space for large tents and a family game of French cricket. The facilities here are in keeping with the campsite's pared-back, partially wild approach. Wonderfully crafted wooden huts contain three composting loos and you can borrow solar-powered shower bags if you want to forgo the regular shower facilities on site. The result is a simple, traditional camping experience on a site as populated by wildlife as it

is by people. Woodpeckers bounce along the tree line, while buzzards can be spotted overhead. A small stream also runs past the meadow – trickling almost dry in the height of summer – beyond which children can play hide and seek in the shady wooded copse.

Those who appreciate such bucolic surroundings yet look for more comforts than the wild camping that's on offer, can take advantage of one of the site's glamping options, ranging from a sturdy shepherd's hut and a cluster of bell tents to some more quirky and innovative options. There is, for example, a tree tent, suspended by taut cords among the trees in one corner of the site, while the well-named 'Hammock Hut' is a wooden Wendy-house-style structure with two hammocks. Each comes with a firepit area for evening campfires, while regular campers can borrow firepits to get in on the marshmallow action.

When daylight returns, Wardley Hill is poised to enjoy the best of Norfolk and Suffolk. The Waveney River leads into the Broads – you can enjoy it drifting by canoe, kayak or sailing boat – and on its banks are the pleasant market towns of Diss, Bungay and Beccles. Many here, however, are rarely in a rush to go anywhere, kicking back instead to enjoy the pleasures close at hand: nature, seclusion and a crackling campfire.

WHO'S IN Couples, families, tents, dogs (on leads) and small campervans – yes. Caravans and single sex groups – no.

ON SITE 25 grass pitches, 4 campervan pitches, lotus tents and bell tents, a Hammock Hut (sleeping 2), a suspended tree tent (sleeping 2) and a shepherd's hut (sleeping 2–4). Glamping units are individually furnished – see website for details of each. Composting loos, showers, drinking water points and recycling bins. Campfires permitted raised off the grass (and they have firepits available to borrow). 3 ponds turn into dry pits at the end of summer (wonderful to explore) and there's a wooded area across a small stream where you'll find a pétanque pitch and communal fire area. Future plans include a library, communal kitchen and glamping boat (sleeping 2), soon to be completed.

OFF SITE Miles of footpaths and lanes offer peaceful cycling, horseriding and walking. The River Waveney passes 1 mile away, providing the gateway into the Norfolk Broads, with boats and canoes available to hire locally. On the river banks, Bungay and Beccles are both market towns with plenty to offer, including art galleries, great pubs, restaurants, supermarkets, tourist information and lots of independant shops.

FOOD & DRINK There's a wonderful Italian restaurant, The Olive Tree (01508 518147), in the village and a small convenience store with a post office. To the west, in Broome, you'll find The Artichoke (01986 893325), a traditional country pub where dogs and sprogs are both welcome, and which serves good food and ales.

GETTING THERE The campsite is at the top of Wardley Hill Road, a turning off the A143 Bungay to Beccles Road, opposite 'Crossways' countryside supplies store.

PUBLIC TRANSPORT Beccles and Diss are the nearest train stations, from where you can catch an Anglia bus to Kirby Cane. The campsite is also on national cycle route 1.

OPEN All year (bell tents from June–September only).

THE DAMAGE Camping: adults £6, children (4–15yrs) £3. Lotus belle tent £60 per night. Shepherd's hut £75 per night. Tree tent £40 per night. Hammock Hut £50 per night.

clippesby hall

Hall Lane, Clippesby, Norfolk NR29 3BL 01493 367800 www.clippesbyhall.com

Safe, comfortable, highly organised Clippesby Hall is a first-time family-campers' delight. From the mini-golf to the swimming pool, from the well-stocked shop to the family-friendly pub, it's all here, like a posh holiday camp. Hi-de-hi, campers!

Clippesby Hall achieves the near impossible – managing to make a large campsite feel friendly, non-commercial, peaceful and altogether rather lovely. Set in the manicured grounds of John Lindsay's family manor house, the site forms its own little self-contained canvas village. The facilities are pretty extensive, with 115 pitches (many with electric hook-ups), a small outdoor swimming pool, two grass tennis courts, a football pitch, mini-golf, archery courses, two children's play areas, a tree house in the woods, games room, bike hire, shop, café, holiday cottages, pine lodges and even an onsite pub.

You might assume, then, that this place is about as quiet and peaceful as a night on the hard shoulder of the A12. But somehow John and his family have managed to incorporate all these amenities into the grounds of their home while still retaining its unique character and personality. The result is an exceptional campsite with a relaxed, family atmosphere.

The site began life as a market garden, but campers have been coming here since the 1970s. It has gradually evolved at its own pace and today the pitches are divided across several camping areas, each landscaped and spacious enough to avoid any feeling of overcrowding, and named according to their individual characters. Pine Woods is a dog-free space almost entirely surrounded by conifers,

The Orchard has plenty of tree-cover, while The Dell is hidden away in a quiet corner with woodland pitches just for tents. Rabbits Grove is a favourite among younger campers, and the Cedar Lawn has pitches spread out over a gently sloping sweep of lawn beneath a huge cedar, complete with rope swing. There is plenty of space between pitches and some interesting nooks and crannies mean that, even in busy periods, you can still find a relatively secluded space.

Clippesby Hall is the perfect location from which to discover the Broads National Park, a network of rivers and lakes that forms Britain's largest protected wetland and can be explored by canoe or by bike. Clippesby work with local guide, The Canoe Man, and also hire out bikes along with route maps, helmets, locks and repair kits.

Don't be surprised when you are personally guided to your pitch on arrival – it's all part of the service, along with the decision not to put large pitch markers and unnecessary signs everywhere. After all, this is John's home and garden. It's been in the family since his grandfather bought the hall in 1945 and he doesn't want to ruin it by making it look like, well, a campsite. And that's the beauty of this unique place. It doesn't feel like a conventional, commercial campsite. It's more like camping in the delightful grounds of a stately home.

WHO'S IN Tents, campervans, caravans, dogs – yes. Big groups, young groups – no.

ON SITE 115 pitches, spread across 8 distinctive areas, ranging from open grassy spaces to secluded, wooded glades and all-weather pitch areas. All areas, except 'The Dell', have electrical hook-ups. Onsite entertainment includes an outdoor heated swimming pool, grass tennis courts, mini-golf, archery, children's play areas, a games room, bike hire, shop, café and an onsite pub. Facility blocks are dotted around the place and have modern showers, toilets, basins, family rooms and washing-up sinks outside. No campfires permitted.

OFF SITE The Broads National Park is Britain's largest protected wetland, and Clippesby Hall's welcome pack includes a booklet all about discovering the area, including ideas for days out on foot, and by bike, boat or canoe. Potter Heigham, located 4 miles north of the campsite, is home to several boatyards hiring out all sorts of vessels by the hour or day. There are glorious dunes and sandy beaches at Winterton-on-Sea, about 6 miles away, and at Horsey, a few miles north, where you can visit the 19th-century Horsey Windpump (01263 740241) before heading off to see the local grey seal colony.

FOOD & DRINK There's plenty of goodies onsite from Susie's Coffee Shop, Susie's ice-cream hut by the pool, the campsite pub – The Muskett Arms – and the campsite shop. The nearest of many other pubs around is The Kings Arms (01493 368333) 1½ miles away in Fleggburgh.

GETTING THERE From the A47 between Norwich and Great Yarmouth, take the A1064 at Acle (Caister-on-Sea road). Take the first left at Clippesby onto the B1152 and follow the signs to 'Clippesby Hall'.

PUBLIC TRANSPORT The nearest train station is in Acle and from there it's either a long walk or a short taxi ride.

OPEN All year.

THE DAMAGE A pitch and 2 people £12.50–£39 per night. Extra adults £6.50, children £3, under-3s free; dogs £5, hook-ups £4.

the fire pit camp

The Firs, Wendling, Norfolk NR19 2LT   07717 315199   www.thefirepitcamp.co.uk

Nothing beats camping in a gang and this campsite caters specifically to big group bookings. As the name suggests, campfires are a must, but by day it's the long grass meadows, giant-tyre slide and double-decker play bus that keep kids entertained.

On the fringes of the classic Norfolk village of Wendling, The Fire Pit is a family-friendly camping extravaganza, inviting young and old alike to play, create and explore. The main meadow has just 15 pitches, along with a magnificent, two-level Hazel Dome Bender Tent, built using recycled materials and accommodating up to eight people. Alongside, a vast playing field has a 'mud-kitchen', giant tyre slide and a retro double-decker bus for kids to play on while, for the parents, a former warehouse space has been transformed into a funky coffee and cocktail bar. If that's not enough there's even an onsite yoga yurt. After all those tasty espressos you'll be needing somewhere in which to power down.

The real glory of The Fire Pit Camp's smaller and more boutique scale is that it can only be hired in its entirety, meaning that, if you get a big enough group together, the whole place is all yours to enjoy. It's ideal for a large-scale family gathering, offering the chance to get creative and have your own annual mini-festival.

When you do break away, there are plenty of highlights to head to. The site is midway between the pleasant market towns of Dereham and Swaffham, and Norwich is within easy reach. The delights of the North Norfolk Coast, are also just half an hour or so to the north; so there's an offering for every type of holiday – come rain, shine or a cloudy something in-between.

WHO'S IN Glampers, campers, large group bookings and whole site hire – yes. Individual tent bookings, caravans, campervans, dogs – no.

ON SITE 15 tent pitches. No electric hook-ups. The Wren's Nest sleeps 8 with a double and single on the mezzanine level and a single, bunk and double sofa below, plus wood-burning stove, solar lighting and a fully equipped kitchen area. There's a playing field, sports pitch, double-decker play bus and yoga yurt, plus the converted warehouse space with games and pool table. Washing-up area. Family-sized shower room with showers and 3 loos. Communal firepit.

OFF SITE Wendling is a short drive from the North Norfolk Coast and, closer to home, you can visit the Green Britain Centre (01760 726100) in Swaffham, home to the only climbable wind turbine in the world!

FOOD & DRINK The onsite warehouse bar sells organic cakes, cocktails and coffee. Creake Abbey Farmers' Market and the one in Dereham boast some of Norfolk's wonderful local produce. The Greenbanks Hotel (01362 687742) in nearby Great Fransham serves refined local cuisine.

GETTING THERE The campsite entrance is on the main road through Wendling opposite a bus stop. Look out for the double-decker bus in the fields beyond.

OPEN The Wren's Nest is open all year. Exclusive hire May–September and during school holidays (Easter, summer and October half term).

THE DAMAGE The Wren's Nest £180 per night. Add £20 for each of the 15 pitches and the whole campsite is yours exclusively for up to 60 people. 2-night minimum.

karma farm eco camp

8 Fen Bank, Isleham, Ely, Cambridgeshire CB7 5SL 07900 961217 www.islehamfen.co.uk

Walk on the riverside, cycle to Ely cathedral or follow the children's trails at the local nature reserve. The famously flat fenlands have a surprising amount to offer and eco-friendly Karma Farm is the perfect base.

Will Taylor bought the land here a generation ago and built his farmhouse from scratch: a carbon-neutral, turf-roofed dwelling that must have seemed quite revolutionary at the time. The low-impact eco-house sets the tone for the rest of Karma Farm, which straddles the Suffolk–Cambridgeshire border. The campsite occupies a pretty spot by the side of the River Lark, with 40 loosely marked-out tent pitches – visitors can simply stroll around and choose the nook they most fancy. There are also a couple of yurts, furnished with king-sized beds made from the farm's own wood, and a three-berth wood-clad cabin, with its own en-suite facilities.

In keeping with the rustic vibe, campfires are permitted, with wood available at the farmhouse. There's a games field and covered shed for rainy days, plus fridge-freezers to use and a brand-new block of washroom facilities, including a large, gas-powered, shower pod into which you could fit your whole family (or a very friendly group).

But perhaps the best thing about Karma Farm is its location right by the river. A track follows the river for seven miles to Prickwillow, while in the other direction a path takes you to the Jude's Ferry Inn about two miles away – choices to be considered over a breakfast of Will's free-range sausages and bacon.

WHO'S IN Tents, campervans, caravans, groups, dogs – yes.

ON SITE 40 camping pitches, 2 yurts and 1 timber-clad cabin. Campfires allowed. Newly refurbished facilities include 2 toilets, 2 hot showers, 1 solar shower and 1 propane-powered shower pod and wash basins. Indoor games barn. Fridge and freezer for free use. Fishing permits given for River Lark, and bicycles available for hire. Bird hides by the pond.

OFF SITE As well as the walks and cycle rides along the river, and birdwatching on site, both Wicken Fen (01353 720274) and RSPB Lakenheath Fen (01842 863400) are just a short drive away.

FOOD & DRINK The village of Isleham is a 20-minute walk and has shops and 2 pubs: The Griffin (01638 780447) and The Rising Sun (01638 780741), both of which do reasonable food. There's also a relatively upmarket restaurant, The Merry Monk (01638 780900), which Will says is good. You can also walk to the Jude's Ferry pub (01638 712277), a lovely 2-mile stroll along the river.

GETTING THERE Take the A14/A11 and, roughly halfway between Newmarket and Barton Mills, take the B1085 north (signposted Freckenham) to Isleham. Drive through the village, bearing left down Sun Street past the post office, and make a left down Waterside; the site is a mile down the track.

OPEN April–October.

THE DAMAGE Adults £10, children (5–15yrs) £5 and under-5s free. Yurts and cabin from £30 per night plus £10 per person. 20% price reduction for returning customers.

twitey's tipis and camping meadows

Lowe Farm, Hunscote Lane, Wellesbourne, Warwickshire CV35 9EX 07725 944204 www.twiteystipis.co.uk

If Stratford-Upon-Avon's Shakespeare is too high-brow for the kids then a little jousting, muck-slinging and catapulting will liven things up at Warwick Castle. Just make sure no swords or pikes make it back to the campsite.

Cross 14 acres of grass meadows (accommodating a maximum of 15 tents at any one time) with friendly owners who hold a relaxed, camp-where-you-like attitude, and you've got yourself one roomy place to pitch. Throw in some world-class Shakespearean sights, a couple of medieval castles and countryside vistas that inspired some of the world's greatest literature, and you've stumbled upon Twitey's Tipis and Camping Meadows – 'A Midsummer Night's Dream' of a campsite.

"Peace and tranquillity is the order of the day," says the site's owner Michael Twite, who has created an undeniably lovely, back-to-basics campsite. Upon arrival, you'll be presented with a wheelbarrow to help move your kit – a fun experience for the children who get a ride from mum or dad. Everyone who stays at Twitey's appreciates the lack of overcrowding. The flat, mown pitches are well spaced out and hidden in one of the two wildflower meadows, providing a sense of remoteness and seclusion. As the name suggests, tipis can also be rented, and the site's small hamlet of three tipis has been thoughtfully positioned to overlook the meadow; each comes furnished with lanterns, kitchen utensils and logs for a sunset campfire.

As for Warwickshire, it may be just another pleasant English county were it not for the birth of one rather gifted playwright, William Shakespeare, who was born and died in Stratford-upon-Avon, just four miles from the site. Naturally, a host of sights here linked to the great man have become a magnet for tourists, and you can sample some of Warwickshire's glorious countryside by following 'Shakespeare's Way', which replicates the 146-mile route the young writer took on his travels to and from London. The scenery is sure to inspire as the route passes rolling hills, the weaving River Stour and the honey-coloured cottages of the Cotswolds further south.

Shakespeare aside, pooped parents looking for offsite activities to tire out their energy-sapping youngsters also have plenty of choice in Warwickshire, not least at nearby Warwick Castle, which hosts a vast array of family activities every summer. Back at Twitey's Tipis and Camping Meadows, meanwhile, carefree kids usually wear themselves out finding their own fun, playing hide-and-seek in the long grass, or hunting bugs and chasing butterflies, ensuring a sound snooze for the whole family. Busy days, peaceful nights. Life's good at Twitey's... *

WHO'S IN Tents, glampers, kids and well-behaved groups – yes. Caravans, motorhomes and dogs – no.

ON SITE 15 pitches in each meadow, mown within long grass and wild flowers, 3 tipis (2 x 4-bed and 1 x 6-bed). All pitches have their own firepit, and 'tents for hire' are also available. Showers, toilet block, washing-up area, small reception and shop with charging facilities, recycling and gas cylinders.

OFF SITE Warwick is only 6 miles away and boasts one of the finest preserved medieval castles in the country. Built in 1068 by William the Conqueror, Warwick Castle (01926 495421) hosts daily trebuchet firings and jousting tournaments in summer, while the Tussauds Group has filled the sumptuous interior with a range of lively attractions that bring the castle's rich history to life. The oh-so-grand Charlecote Park (01789 470277), home to the Lucy family since the 12th century, is only 1 mile away, on the banks of the River Avon, where you can take a scenic cruise. Surrounded by its own deer park, the house tells the family's stories via their portraits and the unique objects they have collected from around the globe. Head to Wellesbourne Mountford Airfield (01789 842007) to check out the underground World War II museum as well as the resident Vulcan bomber. Finally, the old streets of Stratford-Upon-Avon, with its many Shakespeare-related attractions, are the main attraction of the area – albeit one the kids may feel is a little too educational for the school holidays!

FOOD & DRINK The Kings Head (01789 840206) in Wellesbourne oozes rural charm and rustic character. The picturesque surroundings provide the perfect backdrop for savouring the hearty, seasonal pub food and the carefully nurtured cask ales. Recently refurbished, The Fox (01789 840991) at Loxley serves award-winning food 7 days a week, with a menu to suit all ages and appetites.

GETTING THERE Leave the M40 at junction 15 and head south on the A429 (signposted Stow-on-the-Wold). Past the village of Barford, as you approach Wellesbourne, turn right (signposted Charlecote). Drive through the village until you reach a crossroads – Wellesbourne is to your left and Stratford-Upon-Avon to your right. Drive straight across, onto Loxley Lane and, after a few hundred metres, turn right into Hunscote Lane. After about 100m, turn right into a shared driveway signposted 'Lowe Farm'. Proceed along the driveway for 50m then turn sharp right into Lowe Farm. Follow the drive up until you reach the campsite.

PUBLIC TRANSPORT Nearby train stations include Warwick, Warwick Parkway and Stratford-Upon-Avon. There's also a bus service to within ¾ mile of the site.

OPEN All year.

THE DAMAGE 10m tent pitches (with firepit and 1 car) £28 per night for 4 people. Extra people £5 per night. 2-night minimum on weekends and 3 nights on bank holidays. Tipis from £195 for 2 nights – 2-night minimum all year.

the real campsite

Park Farm, Littleworth, Faringdon, Oxfordshire SN7 8ED 07342 034229 www.therealcampsite.co.uk

Keeping the numbers down to fill just a few spacious pitches and providing each with its own 'en-pitch' toilet is a stroke of genius. But, located between the North Downs and the Cotswolds, it's the landscape that really makes this spot a stunner.

After a number of years running one of England's most highly rated glamping sites, the owners at Park Farm on the edge of the Cotswolds have returned to their camping roots and given their site a name to match. There are no more frills and gimmicks on the farm these days, just simple, back-to-basics camping with stonking great vistas of the unfolding land beyond. In fact, what they've really crafted is a site that brings out the best of both worlds. A campsite it may be, but they've still taken a very boutiquey, individual approach to its creation, restricting the numbers to just eight pitches and providing each spot with its own private toilet. Nevertheless, there's still a genuine feel of wild and simple authenticity about it all, with campfires crackling late into the evenings and the bleating of young lambs waking you softly in the morning.

The meadow itself is set on a 370-acre mixed arable and sheep farm, nestled just on the edge of the picturesque village of Littleworth. Today it is run by Lindsay and Alan, but it has been farmed by Lindsay's folks for four generations and there's a warm enthusiasm for the farm and its location that radiates from the whole family. It's clear that Park Farm is a labour of love. From their helpful, personal approach, you can see how proud they are to keep the family tradition alive, and the extra activities, such as Lindsay's felt-making workshop, are a great way to bring visiting families together.

The fields around are home to 400 ewes and, if you visit in April or early May, you might be lucky enough to see the newborns taking their first wobbly steps. There are also two mischievous pygmy goats and a chicken coop where campers can collect eggs for their morning breakfast, fried over rekindled flames. Peep from your tent at the right times and you can also spy less pre-determined critters – hares, buzzards, red kites and deer.

Perhaps one of the site's best features, however, ever-present and ever-changing through the year, is the view. Each pitch boasts a spectacular vista stretching out from the Upper Thames Valley to the Cotswolds beyond. After enough time spent ogling, you're eventually drawn out, either on foot or in the car. Head towards the historic market town of Faringdon, or Thames-at-Radcot, both within a leisurely half-day stroll. Alternatively, take to your wheels and wind your way to Oxford for days spent lounging in the sun as you drift along in a punt.

WHO'S IN Tents, families, couples – yes. Caravans, motorhomes, campervans, dogs, hen and stag parties and large groups (unless booking the entire site) – no. Advance bookings only; no walk-ins.

ON SITE 8 large grass pitches. Each pitch booking is for up to 6 individuals, 3 tents and 1 car-parking space in the farmyard (extra cars bookable). Each of the 8 pitches has a private toilet with wash basin and cold running water, a standpipe for drinking water, a camp firepit (wood available to purchase) and picnic bench. There are no electrical hook-ups and car parking is in the farmyard to keep the meadow safe and traffic-free. Wheelbarrows are provided to transport your luggage. There are 5 showers (including 2 larger, family-sized cubicles) in a block with underfloor heating, a hairdryer, shaving points and 1 further toilet. There's an undercover washing-up area and lockers available to hire for valuables, with a power point for charging small devices (bring your own padlock). A small honesty shop sells essentials and firewood, with free-to-use freezer for ice packs and a communal fridge. Family felt-making workshops are also run – learn how to make felt pictures from scratch using sheep's wool.

OFF SITE Viewing your surroundings is always a good way to start. Faringdon Folly Tower, a unique 100ft tower built by the eccentric Lord Berners in the 1930s, offers fantastic panoramas of the Thames Valley and, a mile or so further north, Radcot Bridge and Lock is a wonderful spot to stop for a picnic. It's the oldest bridge across the Thames and was the scene of many battles. Today, away from the lock itself, this area of the river is also particularly popular for wild swimming. To the south lies Uffington, home to the famous white horse; a hill figure carved into the chalk escarpment and thought to date back to 1000BC. For more farm fun, kids love Farmer Gow's Activity Farm (01793 780555) in nearby Longcot, which has daily feedings at 11am and 2pm. For something more exotic, spot rhinos, giraffes and zebras at Cotswold Wildlife Park (01993 823006), 25 minutes away. If it rains, the dreamy spires of Oxford are an easy 30-minute drive. Spend a day exploring its 38 colleges, pop into the various museums and visit the labyrinth of boutique shops in the covered market. Or, if the weather does clear up, indulge in a spot of punting (01865 515978).

FOOD & DRINK There's a wood-fired oven available to hire by the day, ideal for pizzas, baked potatoes or cooking joints of homegrown Park Farm lamb (available to buy in the honesty shop). Tripods and cauldrons for campfire cooking are also available to hire. If you're venturing off site, you don't need to stumble far – it's a 10-minute walk to The Snooty Mehmaan (01367 242260), a multi-award-winning Indian restaurant. For something more traditional, The Lamb at Buckland (01367 870484) serves local brews and seasonal and hearty pub food and is a pleasant hour's stroll away (there's a bus that can drop you back). Faringdon town centre, meanwhile, is home to plenty of other eateries. A few doors down, the Faringdon Coffee House (01367 241574) has a handful of outdoor tables – grab a slice of cake and watch the world pass by. The Trout Inn (01367 870382) at Tadpole Bridge is a touch on the pricey side, but worth it for its location on the banks of the Thames, with views across the Oxfordshire countryside.

GETTING THERE Full directions will be emailed to you after a booking is placed.

PUBLIC TRANSPORT It's a 10-minute walk to the nearest bus stop, on the Oxford–Swindon 66 bus route (running every 30 minutes or so). The nearest train station is at either end of the route – Oxford or Swindon. The campsite is located 15 miles from each.

OPEN April–October.

THE DAMAGE From £30–£40 per pitch (maximum of 6 individuals and 3 tents).

cotswold farm park

Guiting Power, Gloucestershire GL54 5UG 01451 850307 www.cotswoldfarmpark.co.uk

Err, hello! Camping with children next to the most popular farm park in the country, with an adventure playground, bouncy 'pillows' and baby animals to cuddle and feed. For families, what's not to like?

Being able to pitch a tent in the Cotswolds is a rare occurrence, so it's somewhat apt that it is possible here – at a rare breeds farm. This place is a huge hit with families as you're next to the popular Cotswold Farm Park, made famous as Adam's Farm by TV presenter Adam Henson, and camping here is a genuine farm experience, surrounded by the sights, snorts and smells of all creatures great and small, from Highland cattle and Gloucester Old Spot pigs to chickens and donkeys. Most campers take advantage of the one-off entrance fee for unlimited visits to the farm park, and kids love the adventure playground and the Touch Barn, where you can cuddle newborn chicks, rabbits and ducklings.

And then there are the views. You're camping in a field on top of a Cotswold ridge, with stunning vistas in every direction. Also, because all the land surrounding you is farmed by the park, you have access to the most amazing footpaths. Even the locals can't believe how lovely it is. Many campers use the site as base-camp for exploring the Cotswolds and its variety of attractions, from chocolate-box villages to the spa town of Cheltenham. And the added bonus? When all the tour buses and day-trippers have left, you and the animals are still here. Albeit you're tucked up in a tent and they're in a stable.

WHO'S IN Tents, campervans, caravans, groups, dogs (on leads and not allowed into the farm park) – yes.

ON SITE Approximately 60 grass pitches, some with electricity, water and waste drainage. There's plenty of room in the field to play outdoor games, but the big attraction is the Farm Park next door. The adventure playground has a zip-wire, bouncing pillows, swings and a maze. And, depending on the month, animal lovers get the chance to cuddle new-born-chicks and feed lambs. The facilities have recently been refurbished and include a disabled and family bathroom. An onsite shop offers BBQ packs including home-grown and local produce, ice-block freezing and camping gas. BBQs allowed, but no campfires.

OFF SITE The main attractions are right on your 'farm-step'. You're surrounded by 1600 acres of farmland, with access to wonderful walks. A one-off entry fee gives you unlimited access to Farm Park.

FOOD & DRINK Adam's Kitchen at the Farm Park offers a hearty cooked breakfast and food throughout the day. Local pubs serving food include The Plough Inn at Ford and the Half Way House at Kineton. Bourton-on-the-Water (4 miles) has lots of facilities, including a small supermarket and bakery.

GETTING THERE Cotswold Farm Park is well signposted from the main crossroads between Broadway and Bourton-on-the-Water. Leave the M5 at junction 9 and take the B4077 to Stow-on-the-Wold.

OPEN April–October.

THE DAMAGE Pitches start at £13 a night.

abbey home farm

Burford Road, Cirencester, Gloucestershire GL7 5HF 01285 640441 www.theorganicfarmshop.co.uk

Organic, free-range, homemade, raw, healthy camping on the farm. The place to come for a whole lot of natural goodness. You'll almost feel guilty for driving here, the place is so green. So why not cycle? Walk? Or glide in a solar-powered plane?

One of the many joys of owning an immense organic farm is that you can put two campsites on it and neither of them need know of the other's existence. In fact, the 1500 acres of Soil Association-certified land at Abbey Home Farm is home to multiple little camping and glamping sites – the main public Green Field campsite and, dotted all over the farm, a four-yurt Eco Camp, a single yurt in the woods and, a whole mile away, an amazing, exclusive-hire hideaway.

Perhaps the best is the aptly named 'Magical Glade', with space for about three small tents or two family-sized ones. Since the wood was only planted in 1991, the trees are still relatively small, giving campers the best of both worlds: sheltered seclusion and sunlight. In the centre of the glade a tractor wheel serves as a brazier, and bags of coppiced ash firewood are available to buy at the farm shop, although in the glade (not in the main camping area) guests are permitted to scavenge their own fuel ('bring your own bow saw'). A discreet compost loo and a water tap complete the fixtures and fittings. To keep it secret and magical, this site has to be booked out in its entirety. If you've got the right number it's well worth snapping up.

Should you find the glade is fully booked, the sociable Green Field site is ideal for families anyway. It's a great spot for children to make friends. From your base you can follow a signposted 30-minute walk around the farm, finishing, if you have any sense, with a long break at the farm shop and café. Stocked to the hilt with homegrown organic goodies, it can cater for your every need and then some.

The woodland yurt and four-yurt eco camp are quite magical, too, merging perfectly into the surrounding landscape. If the kids do get lost roaming amid the thick greenery around the four-yurt camp, remind them just to look to the skyline and search for the brightly painted totem pole nearby. And the signs for the composting loos. And the sculpture in the tree. And finally the grey-green canvas of the yurts themselves.

Indeed, there are plenty of little pathways weaving their way through the ever-evolving farm landscape. Most will ultimately lead you back to the charming café and farm shop, which is also brimming with lots of extra information on all the fun, family-friendly educational courses running during the school holidays.

Abbey Home Farm is not just a beautiful place – it is a living expression of one family's passion. There are quite definitely no food miles here. The organic label is far from being a gimmick or token gesture; this is a farm that has always been at the forefront of the organic farming movement. Organic living isn't just a dream; here it has actually become a reality.

WHO'S IN Tents, small campervans – yes. Caravans, dogs – no.

ON SITE There is a 4-yurt eco-camp a 5-minute walk from the farm shop and café, a single-yurt site 20 minutes from the café, a green-field campsite 10 minutes from the café and the 'magical glade' 25 minutes from the café. Finally, the Special Occasions Field is for exclusive hire (limited vehicle access). Yurts have mattresses, carpets and all the cooking equipment you need and the single yurt has a wood-burning stove. Composting loos, timed water taps and a limited number of firepits are available for hire. Run around the totem pole, head out on a farm tour (bank holidays only) or take part in a variety of courses available (see website for full details).

OFF SITE You are in Roman-remains territory, so it's mosaics-a-go-go: Chedworth Villa (01242 890256) is less than 10 minutes away by car and the Corinium Museum in Cirencester (01285 655611) has one of the nation's largest collections of Romano-British finds, along with interactive displays and the opportunity to dress up as a Roman soldier. For creative kids, the Pick a Pot and Paint ceramic studio in Cirencester (01285 650405) is ideal for rainy days.

FOOD & DRINK The all-organic farm shop and café has all you need: milk and meat, fruit and veg, cakes and even ready-meals. The Catherine Wheel in Bibury (01285 740250), 5½ miles away, does children's meals that aren't your bog-standard deep-fried offerings, and offers top-notch pizzas.

GETTING THERE From Cirencester, head east for the A417. At the A417 roundabout go straight ahead and, after the next roundabout, pass the turning for the A429 and take the next left, signposted 'The Organic Farm Shop'.

PUBLIC TRANSPORT From Kemble train station (7 miles) bus 855 runs to Cirencester, from where it's a 30-minute walk to the site.

OPEN Easter–September.

THE DAMAGE The 4-yurt camp (sleeps up to 18) starts at £595 for a long weekend; single yurt £135 for 2 nights; Green Field campsite £4.50 per night per adult, £2 for under-12s; Magical Glade (maximum 8 campers) is £12 per person per night with a £60-per-night minimum charge.

thistledown farm

Tinkley Lane, Nympsfield, Gloucestershire GL10 3UH 01453 860420 www.thistledown.org.uk

The only thing upstaging the massive camping space, ancient valley views and wildlife-friendly ethos is the campsite's own café. It's difficult to think of any reason why you'd need to leave.

Thistledown is quite simply magical. More than just a beautiful campsite nestled among 70 acres of organic meadow and woodland, it is inspirational too. A dream realised by Richard Kelly, who has years of experience in environmental design and construction, Thistledown has been nurtured since 1993, when Richard began creating habitats for the wide range of local plants and wildlife. For years he ran the site as an environmental learning centre with his son Ryan, before branching out into additional events and opening the campsite's café, which sources ingredients from the local area.

It's easy to locate Thistledown: just head towards a majestic wind turbine located 300m from the entrance. The turbine was one of the first to be erected by Ecotricity, the UK's first provider of mainstream renewable electricity, and is a sign of the campsite's eco-friendly ethos. You can camp in three main areas at Thistledown, with up to 75 pitches available in total. But don't for a minute think that you will be crowded out. The whopping 70 acres available take in trees, undulating pasture, glades of wild flowers, and space – everywhere. Even if there's a big group of noisy kids larking about in one of the pastures, with all the tree-cover it's unlikely you'll even be aware of them.

The top site allows cars and offers camping on pitches individually mown into a pretty elderflower orchard, while the bottom two pastures are car-free, and flanked by woodland offering numerous opportunities for lengthy walks, nature-watching or just some good old-fashioned hooning around. Most pitches have their own firepits and in the evening Richard whizzes by selling wood by the bagful. You can take your own bags when he's not around but are asked not to collect branches from the woods. Picnic tables are dotted around and streams gurgle in the background (rope swings near them offer extra excitement), running down from the top of the site towards an old pond at the bottom.

The café is located in the upper area, home not only to some of the best coffee in Gloucestershire but also a wood-fired clay oven, built by Richard and Ryan themselves. Homemade cakes, cream teas and pastries are on offer, alongside fresh pizzas and slow-cooked meats. Special events are run with guest chefs and new polytunnels are being built to grow more herbs and salads for the frequently changing menu. Really it's an echo of everything else here: a respect for the local area, a little innovation and a bit of hard work to create somewhere that every visitor wants to return to.

WHO'S IN Tents, groups, dogs (on leads) – yes. Campervans – yes (in the elderflower orchard). Caravans – no.

ON SITE 75 unmarked pitches spread across 3 main camping areas: the elderflower orchard (20 pitches), where cars are allowed, and the car-free second (20) and third (35) pastures. The lower pastures are more sheltered and have composting loos, showers and washing-up sinks. The elderflower orchard has events toilets only, but it's a short walk to the facilities in the other fields. Campfires allowed in pre-dug firepits. Numerous walks, a lake and a birdwatching hide. The campsite shop's impressive stock includes local produce and firewood.

OFF SITE Walk to Woodchester Mansion and Park (01453 861541) – an unfinished Gothic manor that's, of course, haunted! The area surrounding Thistledown is also known for its burial mounds. The Neolithic Nympsfield Long Barrow has spectacular views over the Severn Valley as well as internal burial chambers, and Hetty Pegler's Tump is just a little further.

FOOD & DRINK The Fieldfare Café onsite has everything you need. Lamb comes from Thistledown Farm itself, as do the herbs and salads, and all food is locally sourced where possible. Foodie heaven Nailsworth is also 3 miles away, where Hobbs House Bakery sells sublime bread and William's Foodhall is an upmarket deli. Stroud Farmers' Market is open every Saturday 9am–2pm. Good local pubs include The Old Spot Inn (01453 542870) at Dursley, with its own microbrewery, and The Black Horse (01453 872556) at Amberley, which has exellent views.

GETTING THERE From the M5 take the A419 towards Stonehouse. After a mile, at the roundabout, take the third exit to Eastington. Continue to Frocester; at the crossroads on Frocester Hill go straight over. After 300m, turn left towards Nympsfield. At the staggered junction go straight across to Tinkley Lane, signposted Nailsworth. After 1 mile Thistledown is on your left.

PUBLIC TRANSPORT Train to Stroud, then twice-daily bus 5 to Nympsfield. Then it's about a 15-minute walk.

OPEN Weather dependent but usually April–October.

THE DAMAGE Tent £10 per night; adults £8; children (4–17yrs) £4; under-4s free. Dogs £2. Advanced bookings only.

the glamping orchard

Longney, Gloucester, Gloucestershire GL2 3SW 07974 174534 www.glampingorchard.co.uk

They may have been on television but there's nothing too Hollywood about The Glamping Orchard on the banks of the River Severn, where a night beneath the stars is as British as they come.

Set within a three-mile-wide meander in the River Severn, the countryside around Longney could well be considered a hidden treasure. After all, when you're just two crow-flown miles from the M5, you wouldn't expect to find such perfectly peaceful pastures as these. In summer, swathes of golden wheat fields shimmer in a breeze that funnels up the Bristol Channel, while green squares of land sit like oddly shaped patches sewn into an old pair of khaki kecks. These, of course, are the orchard – relics of an era when apples were the county's main trade. Today they make the perfect setting for a campsite.

Nestled among trees still bristling with beautifully ripe Russets during summer, The Glamping Orchard offers a peaceful retreat in the form of two luxury abodes. There's a charming bell tent (sleeping up to five) that includes a wood-burning stove and plush double bed with foldout options for an additional three guests. It comes accompanied by a beautiful bathroom on wheels and a private kitchen hut. Bunting festoons the bell tent's central pole and the hand-painted coffee table has an almost Moroccan feel, while small touches, like the wicker basket of extra blankets, reflect the careful attention to detail making you feel right at home. The second and newest addition to The Glamping Orchard is the

spectacular fully restored 1950s Warwick Knight caravan. Believed to be one of only three left in the world, this 'Rolls Royce of caravans' has been renovated from a relic of the road to a staggering luxury caravan as featured on *George Clarke's Amazing Spaces*. Finished to the highest standard throughout, this unique caravan offers glampers a luxury stay with ample room for a family of four. Inside there's a large, cosy seating area complete with a wood-burning stove, while the kitchen offers plenty of cooking space. The sleeping area is separated by sliding doors so that you can enjoy a drink by the fire when the kids are slumbering. It includes snug bunk pods for them and a comfy double bed for two adults. A charmingly rustic shower-on-wheels is adjacent, as is a compost loo. It's stand-out feature, though, is the elaborate roof garden where guests can stretch their legs or sink into a beanbag, while enjoying views of the River Severn or the starry skies above.

The Glamping Orchard exudes a perfect sense of countrified relaxation. If you're hungry, you're welcome to pick apples from the trees, or to collect freshly laid eggs for breakfast. And is there a more quintessentially rural experience than a horse and cart ride down to the local pub for a pint of cider? After all, when you're glamping in an orchard, it would be rude not to, right?

WHO'S IN Glamping only, so no campervans, tents or caravans. Up to 2 dogs welcome in the bell tent only.

ON SITE The Warwick Knight caravan sleeps 4, with 1 double and 2 bunk beds (all bedding included). The fully stocked kitchen includes gas cooker, hob and grill, fridge and all utensils. An outside firepit doubles up as a BBQ (utensils provided). An initial stock of firewood is provided and more is available from the honesty hut. The private wood-fired shower and sink cabin on wheels is 25m away. There's a private compost loo adjacent to the caravan. The bell tent features a double bed with bedding, 2 single futons and the option of adding an extra camp bed or cot, plus lighting, extra blankets and rugs, and a wood-burning stove. Outside, beneath an awning, are a table and chairs beside a firepit which doubles up as a BBQ. The private kitchen hut is fully equipped with a double-burner gas stove and grill and all the cooking utensils and crockery you could need. They even supply essential condiments (coffee, tea, sugar, oil, salt and pepper) along with a cool-box with ice packs that you can replenish from their freezer at any time. Private bathroom adjacent to your tent comprises a wood-fired shower and sink, plus separate compost toilet. Pet the small farm animals, groom the ponies and collect fresh eggs from the chickens. Horse and cart rides organised by request.

OFF SITE The site is just 5 miles from Gloucester and a lovely short walk from the River Severn. It's also just as nice to walk east to the Sharpness Canal. The Severn is excellent for bird and wildlife-watching, especially as The Slimbridge Wetland Reserve (01453 891900) is located nearby. On the canal you can watch the boaters to-ing and fro-ing, usually from a good pub (see below). You can hire your own boat with Gloucester Narrow Boats (01453 899190). If you'd prefer to stay on land, you can rent a bike (01453 899190) to take on the quiet country lanes. Popular nearby attractions include the excellent Cotswold Wildlife Park (01993 823006) and Cotswold Farm Park (01451 850307) – better known as 'Adam's Farm' from the BBC's Countryfile. For a little culture, try the gardens and country houses of nearby Painswick Rococo (01452 813204), Batsford Arboretum (01386 701441) and Sudeley Castle and Gardens (01242 602308).

FOOD & DRINK The Anchor (01452 740433) in Epney is a great local pub situated on the banks of the River Severn, with beautiful views and serving typical pub grub in large portions. The Ship Inn (01452 740260), located on the canalside in Framilode, has a decked seating area and garden for the children. For the best views, though, try The Pilot (01452 690807) in Hardwicke. Elevated to overlook a long stretch of the Sharpness Canal, it has a great play area for little ones and the service and food are always good. For fabulous cooked breakfasts, light lunches and tea and cake (along with more lovely canal views), The Stables Café (01452 741965) in Saul is another great choice.

GETTING THERE Detailed directions are sent with your booking confirmation. Sat nav will get you to the village and, if the postcode isn't recognised, type in 'Longney'.

OPEN Warwick Knight caravan open all year; bell tent April–October only.

THE DAMAGE Caravan prices £95–£145 a night. Bell tent: 3-night stays from £225 (up to 5 people), 4-night midweek stays from £175.

hiring a campervan

If there's one sure-fire way of spicing up your camping trip it's leaving the family car at home and taking a set of shiny new wheels.

No matter how many years you spent playing Tetris in your youth, packing the family car is never an easy task, especially with rigid cool-boxes, clumsy camping stoves and a collection of fold-out chairs to mould into the boot. Bags are covering the rear windscreen, beach balls are blocking the view and are those someone's knees prodding you in the back?

While nothing beats a classic night under canvas, the compact, ergonomic and economical nature of a campervan gives it a special place in the camping pantheon. While you've been bungee-cording water containers to your roof rack and stock-piling bottles of camping gas, an entire team of engineers have gone into designing the fridge in the latest VW campervan. And with less time spent pitching the tent, a van gives you more time to fully explore the local area, too.

Halfway between tent camping and travelling around in a miniature, moveable holiday home, campervans provide all the fun of a regular camping trip but with added weatherproof insurance and an extra element of excitement. After all, nothing can turn a fully grown adult into a kid at Christmas quite like putting them behind the wheel of a vintage VW campervan.

In keeping with the *Cool Camping* ethos, we've steered well clear of colossal Winnebagos and avoided all things caravan, recommending only the best, independent campervan hire companies in the UK. Small but perfectly formed, these campervans are ideally suited to family holidays on bendy British roads and represent just a few of the companies we recommend on coolcamping.com. Visit our website for more vans, more locations and more road-tripping inspiration.

big tree campervans

Based in a small Perthshire village in the heart of Scotland's 'Big Tree Country', this family-run enterprise has a fleet of eight different vans, with room for five when driving and sleeping space for four. Along with their principal location, the Yearsley family can arrange pick-up and drop-off of the vans at the main airports – Edinburgh, Glasgow and Dundee – so you can head straight off into the highlands. There's a dog-friendly van available too. Bring your pooch along or just steal Bob the affable Big Tree dog.

Bankfoot, Perthshire; 01738 788056;
www.bigtreecampervans.com

comfy campers

This vintage campervan hire company on the edge of the Cotswolds has a pristine collection of antique VWs that have all been fully restored with both impeccable attention to detail and a little modern ingenuity. A small kitchen tightly packed with everything you could possibly need is accompanied by an iPod and MP3-compatible stereo and a modern hook-up for campsite electricity, while an extra canvas hammock allows sleeping space for up to five people. All the vans are original 1970s models, so you'll need to embrace a slower-paced spirit on your holiday, but they beat the rest for style hands down.

Uckington, Cheltenham, Gloucestershire; 01242 681199;
www.comfycampers.co.uk

campervantastic

Founded in 2006 by Steve and Kate Lumley, London-based CamperVantastic has fast become the UK's premier, multi-award winning VW California campervan hire specialists. The well-travelled couple met as keen backpackers and will quickly put you at ease in the vehicles – modern VW California and California Beach campervans with plenty of pop-top space and all the 21st century gadgetry you need. If you've got an active holiday in mind, they can sort you out with family extras, including bike, surf and ski racks, drive-away awnings, luxury bedding sets and more. The only hard part? Avoiding the traffic out of London.

Stanstead Road, Lewisham, London; 020 8291 6800;
www.campervantastic.com

bunk campers

If you want to avoid the classic caravan cliché, then Bunk Campers, who renew their fleet every three years, is certainly the company to use. There's nothing vintage about their eight different vehicle models and, while some are large motorhome-type abodes, the smaller, more compact vans still afford plenty of space for families, too. Already one of the best-known campervan hire companies in Ireland, they have bases in Edinburgh and Glasgow (airport pick-up available) and a depot at London Gatwick.

Five locations across the UK; including Edinburgh, Glasgow, Belfast and London Gatwick; 028 9081 3057; www.bunkcampers.com

van kampers

Van Kampers have just one campervan for hire, a new, Brazilian-built VW that has been designed to replicate the style of the classic 70s model but packs an economical petrol engine inside. The result gets you top prizes for style but also some peace of mind when it comes to reliability. The pop-top roof accommodates a cool platform bed that's ideal for children and teenagers, while the seats below fold down to become a double bed for parents. An extra awning sleeps an additional two people. Best of all, it's just two miles from pick-up in Pembrokeshire to the nearest beach.

Mathry, Haverfordwest, Pembrokeshire; 01348 837994; www.vankampers.co.uk

glamper rv

If you want to pull out all the stops, GlamperRV in the Chilterns is the closest thing you can get to a hotel on wheels though, admittedly, it falls well within the 'motorhome' category. When it comes to the interior, think luxury yacht – leather seats, central heating, air conditioning, a plush en suite bathroom and shiny kitchen. They've even put in a Nespresso machine so you can enjoy the very best morning cuppa. While it may be larger than your standard camper, an automatic gearbox, integrated GPS and a reversing camera make it suprisingly easy to manoeuvre. And, if you still don't fancy driving the smallest roads, the GlamperRV has an in-built garage, too, so you can take your bikes along.

Princes Risborough, Buckinghamshire; 0845 838 6796; www.glamperrv.co.uk

greenways of gower

Oxwich, South Gower, Swansea SA31LY 01792 391203 www.greenwaysleisure.co.uk

After the games room and the adventure playground, make sure there's still energy for the short walk to the beach. Oxwich Bay yawns its sandy mouth towards the Bristol Channel and there's plenty of room in the dunes for more adventures, too.

Ah, the Gower – the coastal jewel in Wales' already resplendent crown. It'll come as no surprise to anyone who has visited the region that this was the UK's first designated Area of Outstanding Natural Beauty. It will also come as no surprise that this part of the world boasts a plethora of camping options – from wild coastal sites via glamping breaks to the holiday-park-opolis, clogged to bursting with statics. Thankfully, Greenways of Gower provides a happy medium that's just perfect both for seasoned and first-time campers alike.

The well-kempt field has space for a maximum of 180 tents, though rest assured the owners are sure to maintain the peaceful atmosphere by not admitting anywhere near this amount. Sure, you'll see a scattering of the aforementioned privately owned statics on your way in, but these are segregated from the main elevated camping field and don't impinge on the stunning sea views. As you'd expect with this kind of well-established operation, facilities are more than adequate. There's an onsite bar, and should your little ones have had their fill of playing ball games in the spacious field, there's an adventure playground and games lounge with all manner of amusements. At its heart, this family-run campsite is run with families firmly in mind.

For mums and dads, there's... well, just look around! This being the Gower, the horizon offers some stunning vistas over Oxwich Bay and out to

the Celtic Sea. The bay itself is a popular spot for bathers and watersports, though you're sure to find a relaxed spot among the sand dunes at the eastern end. Further afield, nearby Oystermouth Castle is just one of the many attractions to visit in this most richly historical of Welsh regions.

All in all, this is a tidy and welcoming campsite that's ideal for both peace and quiet, beachside fun and family days out – all easily achievable from a beautiful cliffside base.

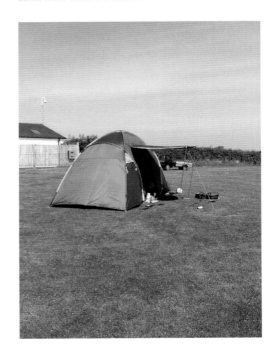

WHO'S IN Tent campers, trailer tents, well-behaved dogs – yes. Large groups, unsupervised under-18s – no.

ON SITE 180 pitches. Modern shower block with underfloor heating, showers, toilets, laundry facilities, sluice, outdoor showers, hairdryers, baby-changing facilities and a disabled-friendly wet-room. Large children's adventure playground, family-friendly bar with children's pool table, air hockey and arcade games. Adults-only snooker room with snooker and pool tables; TVs in both areas. Large camping fields and recreational areas with room for ball games and so on. Campfires are not permitted.

OFF SITE The site overlooks gorgeous Oxwich Bay. The Oxwich Nature Reserve is a designated Site of Special Scientific Interest (SSSI) with an abundance of wildlife, including birds, insects, horses and 600+ species of flowering plants. There is fishing from Oxwich Bay and Oxwich Point, as well as boating, jet-skiing, surfing and kite-boarding. Guests can also enjoy pony-trekking, archery, falconry and some great walking routes in the vicinity – just ask at reception for details and advice. 12th-century Oystermouth Castle is also well worth a visit for anyone with an interest in Welsh history.

FOOD & DRINK The onsite lounge bar serves refreshments, but not food, although plans are afoot to do meals in the future. The King Arthur (01792 390775) and The Gower Inn (01792 233116) are a 5–10-minute drive away.

GETTING THERE From Swansea, follow the A4067 south-west towards Mumbles before turning right onto the B4436, just after the Woodman pub. Follow this road through Kittle and, after 3½ miles, turn right onto the B4436 (Vennaway Lane) for ½ mile. Turn left onto the A4118 towards Oxwich and follow this for 4¼ miles. You will come to an old tower with a road dropping down to Oxwich on the left (signposted). Take this and follow the marsh road for 1½ miles, then over the crossroads and up the hill for ¼ mile. Greenways is on the right at the top of the hill.

OPEN Easter–end October.

THE DAMAGE From £17.50 (1 man tent, low season) to £28 (extra-large 7–10-berth tent, high season).

becks bay camping

Penally, Tenby, Pembrokeshire SA70 7RX 07814 035005 www.becksbay.co.uk

If you like your camping small-scale and simple, then Becks Bay is, as Mary Poppins would say, 'practically perfect in every way'. There's loads of space but very few pitches, and the beach is within spitting distance.

Located within the Pembrokeshire Coast National Park, Becks Bay Camping sits just 100m from the famous coastal path, overlooking the eponymous cove known locally as Becks Bay. In almost every direction the land stretches away in a mass of summer green, while the nearest roads are all shielded by the bushiest of hedgerows. It's no surprise that this sheltered meadow space was destined to become a campsite — it almost seems purpose-built for camping, with just 10 camping pitches, along with four bell tents pitched on flat ground in a tiny wooded glade. There is no electricity, no playground and certainly no Wi-Fi, while the toilets and showers have been newly built into a wooden shed, bodged together with charmingly mismatched wooden doors. The whole place feels thoroughly rustic and, despite having proper flushing loos, still offers a wilder camping experience. This is the sort of spot where children play in rolling fields rather than a playground and campfires crackle through the night. Expect a week or two of getting grass stains out of trousers when you get home.

There are plenty of beaches within reach for when the sun is shining, with Lydstep Bay being the nearest and best known. The National Trust car park here is free and the sands offer excellent views out to Caldey Island, although the giant holiday park that backs it slightly spoils the feel. Instead, head a little further east to Penally Beach — the west end of Tenby's mile-long south beach. Spanning the shoreline from St Catherine's Island to Giltar Point, the views are spectacular. It's slightly quieter than the sandy sections immediately around the town — though all are fantastic, especially if you want to explore Tenby itself at some point during your stay. You can spend the morning on a beach, the afternoon tasting ice creams and the evening back around the campfire. We think that's all the essentials covered.

WHO'S IN Tents, campervans, dogs – yes. Caravans and motorhomes – no.

ON SITE 10 grass pitches and 4 pre-pitched bell tents. Hot shower, flushing toilets and a washing-up area. No electrical hook-ups. Campfires and BBQs permitted.

OFF SITE The campsite is right on the edge of Pembrokeshire Coast National Park with easy access to footpaths, including trails down to the nearest beaches where you can link up with the famous coastal trail. The Manorbier peninsula offers some of the most secluded sandy beaches both east and west of the main surf beach – Precipe and Swan Lake Bay are particular local favourites. Nearby Tenby is an excellent old walled town, with a harbour and expansive beaches at low tide. For something non-beach related, drive 5 miles south-west to Manorbier Castle (01834 871394) a Norman keep located in a beautiful old village. The curtain walls and towers are now partially ruined but well worth a visit. Along with the castle, there are also gardens, a dovecote and a mill to explore.

FOOD & DRINK It's a 2-minute walk to the West Coast Arts Café (01834 219128) and a further 10 minutes to Waves Italian restaurant (01834 870085). The bright blue painted Cross Inn (01834 844665) in Penally is a mile away and has a fantastic, traditional, seaside atmosphere. The Plantagenet (01834 842350) in Tenby is a high-end option in a romantic 10th-century building.

GETTING THERE The campsite is a mile from Penally railway station. Coming from Tenby, the train station is on your left. After a mile the road bends under the railway line and the site is the first and second gate on the left after the bridge.

PUBLIC TRANSPORT Penally railway station is 1 mile away.

OPEN April–November.

THE DAMAGE £8–£10 per adult, £4–£5 per child (2–18yrs), under-2s and dogs free. Bell tents £65–£75 per night, with a minimum stay of 2 nights. A carbon off-set scheme means that for each booking a tree is planted.

point farm

Dale, Haverfordwest, Pembrokeshire SA62 3RD 01646 636842 www.pointfarmdale.co.uk

Like nippers on Christmas Day, you need to be prepared for a very early start to enjoy the gift that is Point Farm Campsite. Book early enough, though, and you can bag a pitch at this teeny, tiny campsite and beat the Pembrokeshire crowds.

It was some time ago that *Cool Camping* first discovered 'the Pembrokeshire paradox'. If we were scholarly types no doubt we would have written a few academic papers on it by now. Pembrokeshire, you see, is a county of unbeatable beauty, home to one of the UK's most enchanting stretches of coastline. Yet, while it offers charmingly peaceful countryside away from the rush of modern life, its tiny towns and villages positively burst in the summer months. What a joy it is, then, to discover Point Farm Campsite. Situated on the Dale peninsula, the county's remote tip, where the cliffs wind in every conceivable direction, Point Farm is a truly tiny hideaway that offers traditional camping in an environment well away from the tourist hype. There are just eight camping pitches and a 'no caravan' policy that gives the whole place a nostalgic, traditional vibe. It's a teeny tiny paradise that epitomises what *Cool Camping* is about, right down to the encouragement of campfires.

The campsite is actually a relatively new venture – a family affair run by Nia, Fil and their two children – although the farm itself dates back to the 1720s. It sits proudly up on top of a gentle slope and boasts panoramic views not just out across the sea but also back inland to the Preseli Mountains and up the Milford Haven estuary. There are two types of pitch: four all-weather pitches with a gravelly base suitable for campervans, with electrical hook-ups and space for cars to be parked alongside, and a slightly lower, terraced grassy space left for tent campers only, their cars parked in an adjacent parking area. There's also a newly added shepherd's hut with a kitchen, beds and all you need inside, suitable for a family of four. All areas are just a few footsteps from the wooden shower block, with a family shower room and a washing-up area, while in the opposite direction you can tumble down through the trees directly onto the Pembrokeshire Coast Path that runs right next to the site. As a walker's stop-off point, it's ideal.

Even if you don't have the legs for the full 186-mile coastal route, though, you needn't worry: provided you can make the first 400m from the campsite you'll find yourself in Dale village and the first en-route pub.

Dale itself is a quaint village fronted by a beautiful sandy beach and is a convenient hub from which to plan your stay – whether it's by renting a surfboard from one of the waterfront shops or planning a kayaking trip up the Milford Haven estuary. You can also hop on a boat for the ferry journey out to Skokholm and Grassholm islands, the former a rugged place noted for its impressive cliffs of red sandstone, the latter home to some 80,000 screaming gannets. The boats can't land (for that, head a few miles across the mainland for a ferry to Skomer Island instead) but they do stop so you can watch the wildlife.

WHO'S IN Tents, trailer tents, campervans, small motorhomes, couples, families, groups, dogs – yes. Caravans – no.

ON SITE 4 all-weather pitches with electric hook-ups, 3 grass pitches without and 1 shepherd's hut (includes a kitchen, beds, bedding and more – see website for details). Wash-block with family shower room (including baby-changing), toilets and a single shower. Laundry service. Firepits available for hire. A shed houses re-charging points, a freezer and beach toys you can borrow. Free Wi-Fi. Exclusive hire of entire site available.

OFF SITE The Pembrokeshire Coast Path runs directly by the campsite, with a number of circular walks taking in the local beaches – Dale, Watwick, Marloes – and picturesque Dale village, a 400m stroll away. On the waterfront, West Wales Watersports (01646 636642) offers tuition and hire of sailing dinghies, windsurfs and stand-up paddleboards. Or drive to Martins Haven, where you can take the ferry out to Skomer Island Nature Reserve (01646 603123).

FOOD & DRINK The Griffin Inn (01646 636227) in Dale is an award-winning pub offering fresh seafood and an excellently cosy, family-friendly atmosphere. You can also head down to the Dale Yacht Club's restaurant, The Moorings (01646 636362), which is open to non-members for breakfasts, lunch and dinner. The Boathouse Café (01646 636929) is open daily for breakfast and lunches too.

GETTING THERE From Haverfordwest, follow the B4327 to Dale. Follow the road along the seafront, turn left by the Griffin Inn and continue past the pub, passing the Yacht Club and following the road behind the cottages to the left. Point Farm is 350m further, on the right.

PUBLIC TRANSPORT A daily bus service runs to Dale from the nearest train stations in Haverfordwest and Milford Haven.

OPEN Easter–end October.

THE DAMAGE Point Farm is for 'Greener Camping' members only. Membership costs £10 a year and you can pay when booking. Adults cost £8–£10 per night, children (5–15yrs) £6, under-5s free. Hook-ups £5 per night; dogs £2 per night.

shortlands farm

Druidston, Haverfordwest, Pembrokeshire SA62 3NE 01437 781234 www.shortlandsfarm.co.uk

Sea-sickness, scurvy, shark-infested waters. If you're not a fan of the sea you might not like the panoramic views at Shortlands Farm. But there's nowhere better to enjoy them than from this laid-back site, safely situated on the top of a nice dry cliff.

Even in a region with no shortage of stunning views, the panoramic vistas over St Brides Bay from Shortlands Farm are unusually spectacular. The Ledwith family's traditional 29-acre dairy farm at Druidston is a breathtaking, back-to-basics campsite that makes the ideal base for those exploring this unspoiled fringe of West Wales. There's a refreshingly laid-back feel to the site – pitches are informal, with campers free to make camp wherever they please. Perched atop the cliffside, exposed to the elements, there's no better place to watch the sun descend over the Irish Sea.

Distant enough from St David's to avoid the crowds, with secluded Druidston Haven just 10 minutes away, Shortlands is also enviably located for the Pembrokeshire Coast Path – which is accessible from a bridleway at the bottom of the farm. From your tent you can wander across, hop on the trail and stroll down the slope to a large, tidal beach, or walk the two-and-a-half miles south to Broad Haven and Little Haven, where there are further beaches and a clutch of sea-front pubs and cafés to enjoy.

All in all, Shortlands Farm guarantees a friendly welcome and the perfect base for exploring this unspoiled stretch of one of the world's great coastal walks. As any beleaguered rambler can attest, the hospitality of Shortlands' hosts knows no bounds. From complimentary use of the fridge-freezer, to a lend of the brazier for campfires, Kate and family are happy to help and have expert local knowledge of the best places to go. Not that you need to go anywhere. With the best views for miles, Shortlands Farm is the one place you'll want to stick around.

WHO'S IN Tents, small campervans, well-behaved large groups and dogs – yes. They also have a separate Caravan Club site for touring caravans and motorhomes.

ON SITE No allocated pitches – campers are free to choose their own spot in the field. Wash-block with 3 toilets, 3 hot showers, 2 sinks, a baby-changing unit, and a large sink outside for washing-up. Fires are allowed as long as the grass is protected. Firepits available to borrow and logs for sale.

OFF SITE The Pembrokeshire Coast Path is 5 minutes from the farm. Druidston Haven is the nearest of many beaches, just a 10–15-minute stroll away. The medieval ruins and seaside charm of St Davids (Britain's smallest city!) is a 25-minute drive away. You'll find a wealth of aquatic activities to partake in here, including coasteering, sea-kayaking and, of course, surfing. For something a little more sedate, The Gallery at Oriel-Y-Felin (01437 720386) is worth a visit, while a boat trip to Ramsey Island (01437 721721) is also unforgettable.

FOOD & DRINK For fish and chips, The Shed (01348 831518) in Porthgain takes some beating. The Swan Inn (01437 781880) is the pick of the pubs, with a great line in inventive seafood dishes. The Druidstone Hotel (01437 781221) restaurant boasts a decent menu of homecooked dishes and some enviable views overlooking St Brides Bay. For supplies, the nearest shop is in Broad Haven – 5 minutes by car or a 40-minute walk along the coast path.

GETTING THERE From Haverfordwest, take the A487 towards St Davids. Turn left at Simpson Cross (signed Nolton Haven). Go straight over the small crossroads, turn right into the no-through road between a red telephone box and a cream cottage. Go all the way to the end.

PUBLIC TRANSPORT Train to Haverfordwest, then local bus to Newgale, and Puffin Shuttle bus to the end of the lane at Shortlands Farm.

OPEN All year.

THE DAMAGE £7.50 per person per night; under-3s are free.

top of the woods

Penrallt, Capel Coleman, Boncath, Pembrokeshire SA37 0EP 01239 842208 www.topofthewoods.co.uk

A real chance to embrace nature, with birds and wildlife enlivening every acre, and streams, woods and meadows for kids to explore. You'll spend the next two weeks washing grass stains out of clothes and untangling twigs from hair.

It's very easy to get lost at Top of the Woods campsite. Not in the literal sense – owners Soo and Jon give you a map on arrival – but in an airy-fairy sort of way. The atmosphere is so laid-back it's almost horizontal, the flittering of bird and wildlife enlivens every acre, and the light, white-grey wisps of campfire smoke give that essential campsite feel that holiday parks just can't contend with. No, there's something lose-yourself special at Top of the Woods. This is a sizeable patch of land, spread over 27 acres, so campers here aren't exactly short of space; and the gargantuan Ffynone Wood, which flanks the site (much of which is now a designated SSSI) just adds to the bucolic feel.

The varied accommodation comprises a 10-acre camping meadow, with just 12 pitch-where-you-like spots, and a further three glamping meadows, one with five bell tents, another with nine airy 'pioneer' tents, and the last with four boutique safari lodges. All of the glamping options come fully furnished, so you can turn up with little more than your toothbrush. There are no electrical hook-ups, though, which keeps a rustic, traditional atmosphere – something accentuated by the fact that cars are parked by the entrance with wheelbarrows for trucking in your gear.

Popping your head through the tent flaps, it's not long before you find a neighbour – usually of the non-human kind. The woods have the largest resident badger population in West Wales, there are lots of rabbits nuzzling along the meadow edges and, if you're particularly lucky, otters can sometimes be spotted slipping into Afon Dulas, a charmingly peaceful stream that runs along the southern edge of the site.

Once part of the huge Ffynone Estate, the campsite is located on quaint Penrallt Farm, an 18th-century farmstead that still has chickens scratching around outside and three kunekune pigs greying the line between pet and farm animal. Within the old Georgian sheds, housemartins to and fro by day, while a rare breed of bat (the farm hosts five of the UK's 17 bat species) also nests within the eves. Slightly separate from the other farm buildings, a Dutch barn has been converted for campers' use as a covered picnic area. It has tables, hammocks and a stash of games for anyone to use and is a handy place to mull over the mapped-out walking route that leads you through trees to the enchantingly named 'secret waterfall'. There's also a delightful hide-and-seek garden crafted out of living willows by a local artist.

In all, Top of the Woods is a throwback to the past. Like a carefree kid from *The Famous Five*, you can delve into the woods in search of adventure or play cricket in the meadows and picnic in the sun. The Pembrokeshire location may often be the thing that brings people here but, by the time they leave, many find they've hardly left the campsite at all, such is the sheer space to get lost in!

WHO'S IN Tents, dogs, groups (by arrangement), gazebos (for a small charge) – yes. Caravans, campervans, trailer tents – no.

ON SITE 4 boutique safari lodges, 5 bell tents, 9 'Pioneer Camps' and 12 meadow pitches. Water points, recycling bins and composting toilets dotted around, plus facilities in the main courtyard – showers, toilets, washing-up sinks, free Wi-Fi and a communal firepit. Dutch barn communal area with picnic tables, phone-charging, games, hammocks, ice-pack freezer and microwave for baby food. Additional showers in the pioneer camp and safari lodge meadows. See website for specific glamping furnishings and details. Campfires permitted off the grass (logs and charcoal for sale). The site has 3 kune-kune pigs, chickens, a dog and a cat. Activities include yoga, bushcraft, campfire storytelling, forest kids club and more.

OFF SITE The campsite sometimes runs events, like guided wildlife walks, through the adjoining 325-acre Ffynone Wood, and maps are provided on arrival with local routes, including Soo's Secret Waterfall Trail. Further afield, attractions include Cardigan Castle (01239 615131) and The Welsh Wildlife Centre in the Teifi Marsh Nature Reserve.

FOOD & DRINK The site offers hot breakfasts at weekends, campfire stews on Fridays and BBQ nights on Saturdays. Food can also be booked in advance, so dinner is ready on arrival. A fishmonger visits twice weekly. Pub-wise, there are 2 good locals: The Nags Head (01239 841200) in Abercych and The Ffynnone Arms in Newchapel (01239 841800).

GETTING THERE From Carmarthen, take the A484 to Cenarth, then the B4332 for 4½ miles. After Newchapel, pass the gatehouses of the Cilwendeg Estate and take the left turn immediately after into Capel Coleman Road. Continue until you reach the small church in St Colman. Take the left fork and continue to the bottom.

OPEN Spring bank holiday weekend–end September.

THE DAMAGE Camping £20–£25 per night, including 2 guests, a car and up to 2 dogs. Extra adults £10, children £5 (3–14yrs), under-3s free. Bell tents from £55 a night, pioneer lodges from £70, eco boutique safari lodges from £90.

sloeberry farm

Crynga Mawr, Blaenannerch, Ceredigion SA43 2BQ 01239 571013 www.sloeberryfarm.com

Getting back to nature doesn't mean giving up every modern luxury – as Sloeberry Farm shows. But there are some that you certainly won't need here. Put down the iPad, switch off the Kindle, confiscate their phones and let the kids loose.

Planning a glamping site may seem simple at first – buy some land, add some accommodation, fill it with the most luxurious items that you can find and install some plush facilities. But the reality of blending these comforts with the back-to-nature camping ethos is easier said than done. How refreshing it is, then, to find a site as subtly sublime as Sloeberry Farm in West Wales – a place where glamping is done right.

The first thing that strikes you about the place when you arrive is the sheer space of it all. The buttercup-dotted meadows and naturally irregular lines of mature trees seem to have been left to their own devices. Bushes bulge and tiny birds flitter along the hedge lines. For children, the exploration opportunities are endless.

The accommodation, meanwhile, seems to fit the space just as a harmoniously as a herd of cows might have done some years ago. Things seem right. There are six creamy bell tents, with a firepit, picnic table and deck chairs outside, giving it all a very classic look, while two enormous canvas lodges in another meadow are built of wood and a forest-green canvas that camouflages them among the surroundings. The immediate appearance is of a good old-fashioned farm campsite with ample space to roam.

Inside is where the magic happens. Bell tents feature mattresses, duvets, cooking equipment and old-style lanterns, while the canvas lodges have a wonderfully exposed wooden interior with a wood-burning stove, deep red sofas and beds for up to seven people. At the back there's an en-suite washroom and each has its own private shower, plus there's a barbecue for enjoying some al fresco dining on your verandah.

All of the bell tents have access to the toilets and gas-powered showers hidden in traditional-style wooden huts at the bottom of the meadow. There are also plenty of interesting finds dotted around the farm. For starters, there's a small, private lake, glistening delightfully when the sun is out, where you can watch pond skaters darting across its surface and dragonflies zipping overhead. There's also a lovely old, tin-roofed barn in the farmyard, its corrugated metal partially rusted, as if a giant orange crayon has been run along its surface.

From the farm you can join local lanes and footpaths heading down to the coast – it's about a three-mile walk all the way down to Aberporth beach. Or you can drive there and enjoy a walk along the coastal path instead. The choice is yours, but when you stay at Sloeberry Farm you're certainly starting in the right place.

WHO'S IN Glampers, families, couples, dogs – yes. Tents, campervans, caravans, large groups, stags and hens – no.

ON SITE 6 bell tents and 2 safari lodges. Bell tents contain real mattresses, duvets and blankets, gas hob cooking facilities, cold locker, kitchen equipment, firepits, picnic tables and deckchairs. There are modern toilets and gas-powered showers in timber huts and a spacious washing-up area. Safari lodges sleep up to 7 people in a king bed, full-size bunk beds, comfy camp bed and a king-size cabin bed. They have leather sofas, wood-burning stoves, a dining table and a fully equipped kitchen including a cold locker. Each lodge has a private shower room and en-suite washroom with basin and flushing toilet, plus a deck with deckchairs and bean bags, picnic tables, firepits and a BBQ.

OFF SITE *Lonely Planet* recently voted Cardigan Bay 'the best place to be in the world' – and no wonder: the cliff walks on the coastal path, sandy bays and National Trust-owned beaches are just the highlights. By car, the town of Cardigan is not far away, formed around a Norman castle, which is open to the public and boasts a great café and frequent outdoor events. Nearby Cilgerran Castle (01239 621339) also welcomes visitors.

FOOD & DRINK The nearest pub, The Penllwyndu Inn (01239 682533), is an easy 1½-mile walk away (don't be put off by the hangman's noose sign!) The next nearest options are either in Cardigan (5 miles) or Aberporth (3 miles). The former has plenty of choice, plus a supermarket for supplies, while the latter is slightly smaller but has a great fish & chip shop (01239 811003) next door to The Ship Inn (01239 810822).

GETTING THERE Sloeberry Farm is very close to Aberporth and easily reachable from the M4 or the main A487 coast road. Full directions given upon booking.

OPEN March–December.

THE DAMAGE Bell tents from £75 (2-night minimum stay). Lodges from £125 (2-night minimum stay).

naturesbase

Tyngwndwn Farm, Cilcennin, Lampeter, Ceredigion, SA48 8RJ 01570 471795 www.naturesbase.co.uk

Nature versus nurture? There's no need to get into this old debate at Naturesbase, a gorgeous natural environment nurtured to perfection by its caring, sharing owners. So, come and help yourself to a hefty chunk of nurtured nature – and a slice of pizza, too.

In his day job, Gyles teaches sustainability, designs school grounds and leads expeditions around the world so, as campsite owners go, he's more than well equipped to steer the verdant helm of Naturesbase with his green fingers. Another Ceredigion-based eco-campsite, the dreamy, clover-and-buttercup-covered meadows at Naturesbase have just 12 pitches – each in their own little mown spots among the wild grasses and flowers. Two of the pitches are taken up by pre-erected safari tents, which afford campers the added luxury of laziness: just turn up and settle in for the night without so much as touching a tent peg. The site caters perfectly for children, with a nature trail to follow, a willow den, animals to feed, a mini football pitch, streams to hop across and a great hill fort to play on. There is also a large indoor play barn with table football, sandpit and skittles. And then there are Gyles' campfire nights: everyone sits around the huge firepit near the communal hub for sing-songs and chats after having their fill of homemade pizza. The kids get to help make the pizza before watching it brown and sizzle in the clay oven. The atmosphere here is unbeatable: tranquil and restorative, but happy and friendly too. There is plenty of space for everyone to have their fair share of nature around here, as well as inviting communal areas in which to chill, sing, play and scoff your pizzas.

WHO'S IN Glampers, campers, tents, dogs (on leads), family groups – yes. Campervans, caravans, single-sex groups – no.

ON SITE 10 grass pitches and 2 safari tents. Campfires permitted. Wash-block with compost loos, flushing loos, 5 hot showers and a family/disabled wet-room with baby-changing facilities. Washing-up sinks, recycling bins and a playbarn with table football, sandpit, scooters to borrow, toy cars and trains, sofas, chairs, board games and books to borrow. Honesty shop stocked with all sorts, from homebaked cakes to hand-drawn postcards. Kids can accompany Gyles feeding the pigs and chickens. Campsite-run pizza nights and communal campfires.

OFF SITE Just half-an-hour's drive away are the sheltered sands of Llangrannog Beach – a beautiful spot with plenty of amenities, so very family-friendly. There is a good dog-walking beach about 5 miles from the site (Cei Bach beach).

FOOD & DRINK Cooked breakfasts available on Mondays and Fridays in the old goat barn. For eating out, Aberaeron's Harbourmaster (01545 570755) is hard to beat.

GETTING THERE From Lampeter, head west on the A482. After a mile, past Felin Fach, take a right (signposted to Ty Mawr Hotel). Follow the road to a T-junction; turn right, then left just before the Cilcennin village sign. Follow the road for a mile and Naturesbase is on the right.

OPEN Mid July–start September. Full-week bookings only during August.

THE DAMAGE Tent, plus 2 people and a car £25 per night. Extra adults £12, children (4–16yrs) £6, under-4s free. Dogs £2. Safari tents (sleep 2 adults, 2 children) from £295 for 3 nights. Lodges are also available.

wild mountains

Cwmdu Village, Carmarthenshire SA19 7DY 07738 284594 www.wild-mountains.com

Peaceful, private and perched in a meadow just outside a pleasant village pub, Wild Mountains is only wild when you want it to be. The stream, the mountains and the wildlife are all out there, but each bell tent has plenty of homely comforts, too.

In the tiny village of Cwmdu, there's a small, honey-coloured building that has been at the heart of the community since the moment it was built back in the early 1820s. The uneven walls run from one terraced section across to the next, connecting a whole row that has, over the years, boasted each and every trade a village could require: It's been a post office, a grocery store, a tailor and linen draper and, of course, a village pub. Indeed, in the 1860s, it was all of these things at the very same time.

Today, Cwmdu Inn, owned by the National Trust and run by the community, retains its essential character – low interior beams, an old inglenook fireplace and a cluster of tables with room for just 17 people – while the home-brewed beers they used to craft in the back room have been replaced by award-winning local ales. Those with a nose for a proper old pub won't be disappointed. And neither will avid campers. For years people have been posting across the internet – where's the nearest campsite? Is there anywhere to camp near Cwmdu? Does the Cwmdu Inn have a campsite? Finally, a happy 'yes' is the answer. And what a campsite it is.

Run by Tom and Lisa Corcoran (and their amiable dog Ambrose), Wild Mountains is not actually owned by the inn but, set in the meadow opposite, it remains very much connected. In fact, it's not exactly a campsite either. Just four pre-pitched, fully furnished bell tents make up the onsite offering, so you can't simply rock up with your own tent or campervan. Inside each you'll find proper mattresses, bedding and a wood-burning stove provided. This is camping in comfort and the small scale of the place lends it real privacy. It's appropriate given the size of the tiny settlement. On the edge of a designated Dark Sky Reserve, it's also blessed with the darkest and starriest of night skies, so setting some time aside for stargazing is a must.

From your tent there's ample space for the littl'uns to go exploring. Mature trees and hedgerows hug the meadow in a green embrace, while the River Dulais skirts along one side. On a hot day, children delight in dabbling along its edges, building makeshift dams. Ruined Talley Abbey is also within walking distance – a fair trek but a pleasant, countryside one – and by car there is a wealth of castles and heritage attractions in the vicinity. As the name suggests, though, it's the rural, remote aspect of this campsite that is the real appeal. The Black Mountain and Llyn Y Fan Fach lake in the nearby Brecon Beacons National Park awaits any would-be explorer, with long days in the outdoors only accentuating the pleasures of the cosy pub at the end. It's a ready-made itinerary that never gets old.

WHO'S IN Glamping only. Additional tent pitches, caravans or campervans – no. Dogs – yes.

ON SITE 4 bell tents (furnished with beds, bedding, cushions, blankets, wood-burning stove and storage), 3 showers, composting toilets, covered communal shelter with electricity for charging phones, drying hair, etc. There is no mobile phone signal on the site but the pub has free Wi-Fi.

OFF SITE There are several excellent walks directly from the campsite (bring an OS map to make the most of the area). These include a 40-minute stroll up to the ruin of Talley Abbey and a jaunt around Talley Lakes and Nature Reserve. Dinefwr Castle and Carreg Cennen Castle (01558 822291) are both less than 30 minutes away by car and the National Botanic Gardens of Wales (01558 667149) are also 30 minutes away. For something a little more high-octane, mountain biking in Brechfa Forest offers trails for various levels of ability.

FOOD & DRINK Hampers filled with local produce are available. The pub is open Wed–Sat, with food served on Saturdays. Beer is mainly supplied from the Llandeilo-based Evan Evans brewery, with a range of award-winning ales. The Cwmdu shop and post office stocks local produce (open Tues–Sat, mornings only). In Llandeilo there's also a popular chocolate and ice-cream parlour that the kids will love – Heavenly (01558 822800). For a hearty Sunday lunch, head to The Plough (01558 823431) in Rhosmaen.

GETTING THERE On the north edge of Llandeilo, leave the A40 on Talley Road (B4302). Follow this for 5 miles where you will see a sign for Cwmdu on the left. Follow the road for a mile to the pub. Wild Mountains is past the pub, down an access track.

OPEN Late March–early October.

THE DAMAGE Bell tents £60–£80 per night. 50% of payment required upfront.

dinas: hideaway in the hills

Dinas Caravan Park and Camping, Llanbedr, Gwynedd LL45 2PH 01341 241585 www.hideaway-in-the-hills.com

Dino, Dinas, Dinam? No, it's not Latin, it's Welsh, but it's the second part of this campsite's name you want to focus on. 'Hideaway in the Hills', is a very apt description. Just make sure you take the map book to find it.

With a name like 'Hideaway in the Hills' expectations of Dinas campsite were high. Thankfully, they didn't disappoint. It is accessed by narrow roads and nestled in a picturesque Snowdonian valley, so you really do feel like you've stumbled upon a hidden gem.

Small, quiet and family-friendly, Dinas caravan park is on mostly level ground, split between the stream-side lower field and the upper field, and surrounded by tall oak trees. Each pitch comes complete with its own picnic table. Campfires are, of course, what really add the 'cool' to camping, and here they are enthusiastically encouraged. For just a couple of quid you can hire a metal firebox, then you're good to go. Firewood is helpfully brought around each evening and once those flames are flickering you can indulge in some scrumptious S'mores - toasted marshmallows with melted chocolate, sandwiched between two biscuits (see p129). Sit back and enjoy the sugar rush.

Dinas is truly a place of peace, and as such the owners ask that noise is kept to a minimum between the hours of 11pm and 7.30am, with loud music being a no-no. All this adds to the tranquil vibe and helps everyone get a good night's kip. In any case, you will want to get up early, as this truly is nature's playground – kids will be entertained for hours building dens in the forest, dams in the stream or playing on the rope swings. The campsite

also has its very own lake where you can hire a Canadian canoe and take to the water. If you like your camping a little more deluxe, then Dinas also offers glamping in the form of a pre-erected bell tent complete with double bed, duvet, pillows and even a television! Somewhere in between this and a regular tent is the camping pod; you won't be sleeping under canvas as it's made of wood (and even has a carpet), but it's not too far removed from an authentic camping experience, and feels a bit like sleeping in a snug den.

In truth, you could quite happily spend your entire stay without venturing outside the campsite, but you would be missing out on the special treats the area has to offer. The nearest beach – Llandanwg – is only three miles away and has views across the peninsula and rock pools to explore. Shell Island, as the name suggests, is the place to head for some impressive additions to your crustacean collection and also boasts some of the highest sand dunes in Wales. Morfa Dyffryn beach is another fantastic sandy stretch, in part home to disrobing naturists. Of course, the best way to explore this area is on foot, and the helpful folk at Dinas provide walking guides for leisurely strolls or more taxing rambles in the area. There's also a little hill called Snowdon that's not too far away, either.

WHO'S IN Tents, glampers, families, couples and kids – yes. Dogs and large groups – no.

ON SITE 30 camping spaces, 1 glamping bell tent (fully furnished, including a televison), a camping pod and self-catering caravans. Toilet block and showers. Electric shaving point. Freezer/ice-pack service. Each pitch has its own wooden picnic table. Pay phone available 24hrs. 6 electric hook-ups (lower field). Wi-Fi (upper field). Coin-operated tumble dryer. Canoe hire.

OFF SITE The campsite gives direct access to The Ardudwy Way walking trail, plus there are numerous walks in the Rhinogydd Mountains and, of course, there's the imposing challenge of Snowdon. Get on your bike and head to Coed y Brenin (01341 440747) for some world-class mountain biking trails through the forest, with downhill trails for every level. Popular Zip World (01248 601444) is a firm family favourite, with zip lines across the Snowdonia valleys (including Europe's longest). The same company have also recently opened Bounce Below, ginormous trampolines set within caves and disused mine shafts. Nearby Harlech Castle is a UNESCO World Heritage Site, while Italianate Portmeirion village (01766 770000) is on the tourist map thanks to its colourful buildings, shops and cafés. For an alternative way of exploring the area, travel by steam train on the Ffestiniog and Welsh Highland Railway (01766 516000).

FOOD & DRINK The Victoria (01341 241213) in nearby Llanbedr is a good place to refuel, with decent pub food and good beer. Harlech has a wealth of tea rooms and cafés, including the tasty Llew Glas Deli (01766 781095).

GETTING THERE Llanbedr village, 2.5 miles from the campsite, is situated between Barmouth and Harlech on the A496 coastal road.

OPEN All year.

THE DAMAGE Adults £8–£9; children (3–15yrs) £3.50–£4; under-3s free. Glamping from £125 for 2 nights.

gwerniago farm

Pennal, Machynlleth, Powys SY20 9JX 01654 791227 www.gwerniago.co.uk

Is it a pirate castle? Or a soldier's battalion? A fairy glen? A princess's tower? Don't tell the kids, but it's actually a rocky outcrop protruding from the camping field that they'll just love exploring – making this the perfect place to play out a childhood dream.

What makes a perfect campsite? Quiet farmland location? Nearby beach? Friendly owners who like campfires, children and dogs?

Gwerniago Farm has all of the above and a lot more besides. Located in the pretty Dovey Valley, it's a large field divided by the natural boundaries of a spreading oak and rocky outcrop – a pastoral paradise for children to run around and discover. The family have farmed here for three generations now, so camping here gives you a great insight into a farmer's working life. Arrive at tea time and you might see farmer Trevor's sheepdog herding his flock back out to their field, with Trevor opening gates ahead of them on his quad bike.

The owners will lend you fire baskets for campfires, which you can have beside your tent. As wisps of smoke drift skywards and marshmallows bubble in the heat, the hustle and bustle of urban life seems a long way away; it'd be all too easy to spend several days here without feeling the need to leave the site at all. But that might be a shame as the beach and little harbour at Aberdyfi is less than a 15-minute drive north, and there's also the seaside resort of Borth to the south, with its pebble beach and laid-back surf dudes. There's even a family-friendly pub in the village, within walking distance down a quiet lane.

You can't really ask for much more than that, can you?

WHO'S IN Tents, campervans, caravans, dogs – yes.

ON SITE One field divided into 3 sections with non-electric grass pitches and grass and hardstanding pitches with electrical hook-ups. A modern facilities block has toilets, shower rooms, a family room with shower and bath, and a disabled room, plus a small kitchen with a washing-up sink and fridge and freezer units. Wi-Fi available. In the evenings, rides can be arranged on Sophie the Welsh mountain pony (£2 a ride).

OFF SITE Plenty of seaside activities at Borth, where the pebbly beach is a good surf spot; in summer there are lifeguards. Down the coast is Newquay, with daily cruises to spot dolphins, harbour porpoises and grey Atlantic seals. North of Pennal, the Centre for Alternative Technology (CAT; 01654 705950) is popular with all ages.

FOOD & DRINK Try the homity pie at CAT for a meal with a small carbon footprint and, if you're in Machynlleth, the Quarry Café does good vegetarian food (01654 702624). There's a nice little coffee shop at Borth called Oriel Tir a Mor Gallery (01970 871042) – ideal if the weather is grim.

GETTING THERE Turn right by the clock in Machynlleth, over the bridge, then immediately left. Follow the road for 2 miles. You will see a site sign on the left-hand side. Take that little road and the site is the first farm on the right.

PUBLIC TRANSPORT Take a train to Machynlleth then bus 29 (towards Tywyn), which stops at the bottom of the lane.

OPEN March–November.

THE DAMAGE £15 per grass pitch, £19 for electric (both include 2 people and 1 car). Extra adults £5, children (2–16yrs) £3, under-2s free. Large groups should ring in advance.

fforest fields

Hundred House, Builth Wells, Powys LD1 5RT 01982 570406 www.fforestfields.co.uk

A vast, well-managed, award-winning campsite with trees to climb, hedgerows to hide in and streams to trace through the greenery. Where do they lead? To the beautiful boating lake, of course!

Despite tents and caravans speckling the meadows and children swimming in the lake, humans tread surprisingly lightly at this 100-pitch campsite in Mid-Wales. The lake may be manmade, but it has been done with such care and taste that even Mother Nature herself would surely give it her blessing. And if you stand in the middle of this campsite and spin around, the natural scenery that greets the eye is simply breathtaking – rolling hills in every direction, forests thick with pine trees, grass, ferns, heather and crystal-clear streams. The best bit is that you're free to wander off in any one of these directions, because the land (all 550 acres of it) belongs to Fforest Fields.

There is so much walking to be done here – over the hills, through the forests and across the moorland. Maps are available at reception and there's a six-mile waymarked walk to Aberedw village that's well worth doing, not least because it winds up at a terrific pub. The long fishing lake offers more sedate activity and its cool waters also make for refreshing swimming or canoeing in one of the site's kayaks. So the chance to commune with nature is at an all-time high. In fact, not far away at Gigrin Farm in Rhayader, there's also a red kite feeding centre, where you can get up close and personal with these majestic birds of prey.

While nature abounds, there are plenty of opportunities for the human spirit to shine here too, not just through tree-hugging and skipping barefoot across the grass, but also through old-fashioned trust. Campers are welcome to help themselves to locally produced food – sausages, organic milk, cheese, eggs, bread and more – and use the laundry facilities as long as they pay a contribution into an honesty box. There are fridges for all to use, homemade firepit structures you can borrow to melt marshmallows on, and games and books if it happens to rain. It's a 'share and share alike' ethos that makes for friendly, sociable camping.

The main facilities – toilets, showers, sinks and so on – are all housed in a new, timber-framed building with solar panels on the rooftop and a vast amount of space inside. It's kept warm entirely by the campsite's own firewood and has underfloor heating throughout. The showers are excellent; cubicles are large and there are separate family rooms and disabled facilities. No surprise, then, that Fforest Fields was *the AA's* 'Welsh Campsite of the Year' in 2016 – it's testament to the perfect marriage they have made here between the campsite and its surroundings. Some people return year after year, including one man who returned to the same pitch every year until he reached the grand old age of 85 – a Cool Camper indeed! Unusual? Perhaps. But, once you've visited, who knows how many times you will return?

WHO'S IN Tents, campervans, caravans and dogs (on leads at all times) – yes.

ON SITE 100 camping pitches, 2 yurts (sleeping up to 4 each) and 2 safari tents (sleeping up to 7 each). Glamping options are fully furnished (see website for details). There's a beautiful timber-framed loo and shower building with underfloor heating, separate family rooms and a fully dedicated disabled room, each with plenty of space. The laundry/baby-changing/washing-up room contains 3 sinks for washing-up and 1 for clothes, 2 washing machines (£3 per wash) and 2 tumble dryers (£1 per half an hour). There's a telephone box and campers' room behind reception with 2 fridges and 2 freezers (cleaned out every Monday and Thursday), microwave and 6 charger boxes for phones/cameras. These are cunning devices – little lockable tins attached to the walls, with room enough for the charger cables to stick out and be plugged into the wall sockets. They are free, but if you lose the key it's a £20 fine. Games are available to borrow, as are BBQs/firepits, and wood and charcoal are for sale in reception.

OFF SITE Head into Builth Wells for a look around the town; if you fancy seeing a film (or perhaps a play, if one's on) there's the Wyeside Arts Centre (01982 552555), which also has lectures on a variety of topics. For something a bit different, there's the National Cycle Collection (01597 825531) at Llandrindod Wells, 8 miles to the north of Builth Wells – a bicycle museum with hundreds of different bikes, the oldest of which dates back to 1819. Those wanting to do a bit of biking themselves should head for Coed Trallwm mountain-biking centre at Aberwesyn, north-west of Builth Wells (01591 610546), which has 3 graded trails of between 4km and 5km in length and a small café – though you'll need to bring your own bike. To see red kites close up visit Gigrin Farm in Rhayader (01597 810243). Finally, if you're lucky enough to be here during August, you may catch the excellent and renowned World Bog-Snorkelling Championships, which take place over the bank holiday every year at a peat bog just outside Lanwrytd Wells – a truly Welsh institution if ever there was one.

FOOD & DRINK A tiny shop inside reception sells locally made essentials like milk, cream, orange juice, bacon, butter, bread and homemade ice cream, while the on-site Fforest Café sells delicious locally sourced coffee, drinks, snacks and light food (open weekends and peak times). In Builth Wells, the Strand Café (01982 552652) does good breakfasts, lunches and teas, while The Fountain Inn (01982 553920) is a decent boozer with a good choice of ales and an adjoining café. For higher-end food, travel a bit further afield to Lanwrytd Wells, where the Lasswade Hotel (01591 610515) has a fine restaurant serving innovative food at moderate prices. The closest of the lot is The Hundred House Inn (01982 570231), ¼ mile away, with a nice atmosphere and decent food.

GETTING THERE If you're coming from the M5, take the A44 then A481 towards Builth Wells; Fforest Fields is signposted and is on the left, just under a mile from the village of Hundred House. From the M4, take the A40 then A470 to Builth Wells, pass through the town, then at the roundabout take the third exit onto the A481. Fforest Fields is a few miles down the road on the right and is signposted.

OPEN Easter–end October.

THE DAMAGE Pitches £4.50, adults £4.50, children (3-16yrs) £3, under-3s free; hook-ups £3, dogs free (max 2 per tent or campervan). Yurts and lodges start from £110 per night.

gold acre

Yarpole, Leominster, Herefordshire HR6 0BA 07907781961 www.gold-acre.com

Don't be fooled; this place is more than an acre in size. In fact, Gold 12-Acre, as it should be known, has enough space to host a camping village. But by purposefully keeping the numbers low, this spacious spot retains a truly exclusive vibe.

There's so much space at Gold Acre, the owners could have filled the meadow with tents and had their own miniature festival – a fitting idea given that the Hay Festival, Ludlow Food Festival and Green Man Festival are all held within half an hour's drive. But that's not the way they roll. Why tarnish such space with festivities? Why knock back the golden grass that gave the site its name? Instead they've decided to keep things simple and blissfully low-key at Gold Acre, with just a single yurt in a quiet corner of a field and a second one on the way, similarly sheltered in its own private space. The outcome, of course, is a glamping experience that's wonderfully private, yet also extraordinarily open, with room to run wild and explore the local area in your own 'holiday bubble'. You're not *always* alone. On occasion a couple of ponies or a herd of sheep will graze in a paddock at the far end of the field. But they're happy to respect your privacy.

The yurt is the genuine artefact, made in Mongolia and hand-painted in the traditional style. Inside it features traditional furnishings, too: rugs, cushions and handcrafted wooden stools, along with a few extra glamping flourishes like the huge double bed. In the centre, a wood-burning stove throws out heat on chilly nights, while the Mongolian felt lining ensures the whole place is well-insulated all year round. Outside, a well-stocked camp kitchen has everything you need

for cooking up a storm, plus a large firepit allows for some Mongolian-style outdoor cooking. For the best produce it's only a five-minute walk to Yarpole, a gorgeous little village with a community shop inside the church.

Beyond Gold Acre, National Trust-owned Croft Castle is within walking distance – a grand stately home treading the line between a castle and a decadently designed country house, that's a wonderful attraction for families who want to explore. The house and gardens have a rich history and a range of insightful events and exhibitions, and, when the little ones bore of such subtle education, you can head out into the vast grounds and tire them out building dens in the woods.

WHO'S IN Glamping only, though an extra tent is often allowed if you ask. Dogs – please ask.

ON SITE A 19ft Mongolian yurt (sleeping 5) that features 1 double bed, 3 single futons, a wood-burning stove, Mongolian furniture, rugs, blankets and lanterns. A well-equipped field kitchen with gas cooker, oven and sink. Campfire with outdoor cooking equipment and cast iron cooking pots. Solar power in the yurt for charging phones and lighting. Outdoor shower and a compost loo. Second yurt available from Autumn 2017.

OFF SITE It's a 5-minute stroll to Yarpole village with a community grocery shop, post office and café all housed inside the church. Recently voted 'best shop in the UK', 40% of its products are sourced from within a 40-mile radius and some are unique to the shop, including their own wine. A mile away, Croft Castle (01568 780120) is set in 1500 acres of grounds and is a joy to explore, with its walled gardens and vast stretches of forest. Events include battle re-enactments, art installations and festivals. Above the castle, the Croft Ambrey hill fort has far-reaching views.

FOOD & DRINK The 16th-century Bell Inn (01568 780537) in Yarpole is a 5-minute walk, while The Boot in Orleton (01568 780228) is another nearby option, serving a traditional Shropshire Sunday lunch. 15 minute's by car, Ludlow has over 50 restaurants and cafés to choose from.

GETTING THERE Leave the A49 at the Wooferton crossroads following signs to Brimfield. Drive through Brimfield and, at the next crossroads, turn left on the B4362. Continue for 2½ miles and turn left for Yarpole just after the sign for Bircher. Gold Acre is 100m further on the left.

PUBLIC TRANSPORT A bus service runs from Ludlow and Leominster train stations to within 100m of the campsite.

OPEN Due to planning restrictions at the time of print, exact dates are still to be confirmed. See website for details.

THE DAMAGE £65–£70 per night (2-night minimum). Extra tents £10 per person per night (children £5).

brook house farm

Wall Under Heywood, Shropshire SY6 7DS 01694 771599 www.brookcottageandcamping.co.uk

Don't be fooled by the perfectly flat, grassy meadows of the campsite; this is the heart of the Shropshire Hills and if you want the best views bring some walking boots along. You can cool off after with a pint in the local pub or a paddle in the brook.

There are plenty of reasons to visit Brook House Farm. Firstly, it's nestled in the middle of beautiful Shropshire countryside, yet still close to the ancient towns of Church Stretton and Much Wenlock. A family-friendly spot, it also boasts a variety of accommodation, from nomadic yurts and glamping pods to traditional tent camping and a few spaces for campervans and caravans. We also love that it's close to so many great things to see and do, and only a three-minute walk to the village pub!

The camping field is home to some very generously sized, immaculately kept, well-spaced pitches, with ample room for ball games and other activities in between. For those seeking a touch of comfort, there are two camping pods – a luxury one and a family one – both of which sleep up to two adults and two children. Each pod comes carpeted, fully insulated and with electric sockets, a USB charging point and LED lighting: perfect for walkers and cyclists who want to rest their weary legs after days exploring the stunning Shropshire Hills. The luxury pod also has storage cabinets, a kettle and small camping stove, a double bed (bedding is extra) and two outdoor reclining chairs.

Despite such seclusion, Brook House Farm isn't too far from civilisation. Spend a week here and you won't run out of things to do; in fact, you'll probably want to stay longer.

WHO'S IN Glampers, campers, tents, caravans, campervans and dogs – yes. Noisy groups – no.

ON SITE 10 grass pitches and 2 hardstandings, all with electrical hook-ups. 2 pods, 2 yurts and 1 unfurnished bell tent (each sleeping up to 4). Wash-block with showers, toilets, wash basins and a washing-up area, waste disposal, recycling and an information board with local attractions. Summer evenings see occasional pancake parties, plus there's a large communal firepit. See website for further glamping details.

OFF SITE The village has a tennis court, playground and sports field. Church Stretton and medieval Much Wenlock, home to an evocative ruined priory, are just a few minutes away by car, as is the foodie hub of Ludlow, with its picturesque centre and castle. But the area's biggest draws are its natural assets – the heathy chunk of the Long Mynd, which dominates views for miles hereabouts, and the limestone escarpment of Wenlock Edge, both excellent for walking.

FOOD & DRINK The Plough Inn (01694 771833), a 5-minute walk away, is a cosy country inn serving local ales and food and hosting occasional live music. Further up the lane – a 40-minute walk – the charming medieval village of Cardington is home to what claims to be the oldest pub in Shropshire, The Royal Oak (01694 771266).

GETTING THERE Turn off the B4371 directly opposite the village hall and the campsite is on the right.

OPEN April–October. Pods all year (except January).

THE DAMAGE Tents £10–£20 depending on size. Caravans and campervans £15. Electric hook-ups £3. Children (6–16yrs) £3, under-6s free. Pods from £40 per night. Yurts from £65 per night. Bell tent from £35 per night.

common end farm

Swinscoe, Ashbourne, Derbyshire DE6 2BW 01335 210352 www.commonendfarmcampsite.co.uk

Stuff nearby Alton Towers – kids make their own fun here. Scale the peaks of the Peak District, discover the dells of Derbyshire and cherish the crackle of campfires. Just one more marshmallow before bedtime...

Alton Towers theme park may be only a short drive away, but this is an unashamedly simple, un-commercial campsite where kids will make their own entertainment. The small, family-run site at Common End Farm has just 30 pitches across a flattish field, with lovely open views over the Manifold Valley across to Dovedale and Thorpe Cloud. With plenty of space for the kids to run around and ride their bikes, you might even get the chance to sit back and enjoy the scenery before being roped in for a game of cricket.

The site is also a great base from which to strike out and explore the southern tip of the Peak District. A two-mile network of footpaths leads you straight from the site to Dovedale, with its iconic gorge and stepping stones. From here you can climb up the distinctive, conical Thorpe Cloud hill, which rises up from the side of the River Dove. Or a two-and-a-half mile round-trip takes you through the tranquil Victorian landscape and woodland at the National Trust's Ilam Park, where you can stop off for a cream tea on the lawn. The historic market town of Ashbourne and the Tissington and Manifold cycle trails are all within three miles of the site, too. So stick your finger on the map and take your pick. There's plenty about to do.

WHO'S IN Tents, caravans, dogs, groups – yes.

ON SITE 16 pitches with hook-ups, 10 pitches without, and an extra overflow field for a few more. Campfires allowed as long as they are contained and off the ground. A stone barn houses 3 washing-up sinks and a freezer for ice packs. Separate block with unisex toilets and a family shower room (includes a toilet, basin, walk-in shower and change table). The road is just off the A52, so there can be some slight traffic noise.

OFF SITE Explore the wonders of Derbyshire and the Peak District. If you hit a rainy day and are visiting with children, the Museum of Childhood (01283 585305) is at Sudbury Hall, around 30 minutes away by car. Around the same distance in the opposite direction is Kedleston Hall (01332 842191). Both are run by the National Trust.

FOOD & DRINK Traditional Staffordshire oatcakes are on the menu and children and dogs welcome at the local Dog & Partridge (01335 343183), half a mile down the road. The Royal Oak (01335 300090) in Mayfield is another good local (with yummy puds) and the Cock Inn at Clifton (01335 342654) has an open fire and traditional pub grub.

GETTING THERE From Ashbourne, follow the A52 towards Leek and continue through Mayfield to Swinscoe. Pass the pub on the left and, after ½ mile, look out for a green sign on the right. Turn right and you're there.

OPEN Weekend before Easter–end of September.

THE DAMAGE From £17 for 2 people with a tent and car. Add £2.50 or £4 per night for 6amp or 16amp electric hook-ups respectively. Adults £5 per night, children (3–15yrs) £3. Extra cars £2, dogs £2 per night.

the royal oak

Hurdlow, Nr Buxton, Derbyshire SK17 9QJ 01298 83288 www.peakpub.co.uk

The only thing that's better than camping in a good, old-fashioned pub garden is when that pub also happens to sell the world's largest and tastiest pies. Who ate all the pies? Ummm. We did.

The biggest challenge for those staying at the Royal Oak isn't wrestling with a sloping camping field (it's flat), being kept awake by traffic (it's not near a main road) or finding things to do (it's slap bang in the middle of the Peak District). No. It's chomping your way through one of the award-winning pies sold at the onsite pub. You could probably actually camp in one of these monsters – they're that big. Packed with fine ingredients, they make a perfect end to a day's play in the Peaks, especially if accompanied by one of the pub's excellent local draught ales.

There are two camping fields here: one sloping and one flat, with space for around 30 pitches (bring strong pegs for the rocky ground in the upper field), and there's a converted stone barn with comfortable bunks if the weather's wreaking havoc. Surrounded by over 100 acres of farmland, with the 13-mile Tissington Trail passing right next to it and the Limestone Way actually cutting through some of the site, this is a great base for those interested in walking and cycling – especially since Parsley Hay Cycle Hire is two miles away and has a range of bikes for adults and kids, including tandems.

Bakewell, Ashbourne, and the spa town of Buxton are all short drives away, making this an accessible and friendly place to get up close and personal with the British countryside – and its pies.

WHO'S IN Tents, small campervans – yes. Caravans – no. Dogs, groups – by arrangement.

ON SITE 30 undesignated grass pitches. Small campfires are allowed if contained and off the ground (firepits for hire). Two camping fields (the lower one is flatter) with good washing-up facilities, free hot showers, and toilets in a barn.

OFF SITE Bakewell (famous for its tarts) has the Pavilion Gardens (01298 23114) and the charming Opera House. Ashbourne and the spa town of Buxton are short drives away. Monyash village has a great park for kids. Parsley Hay Cycle Hire (01629 816200) is two miles away and has a wide range of bikes.

FOOD & DRINK The Royal Oak serves real ales, alarmingly good pies and other award-winning pub grub. The best fry-up in the area is available at the Old Smithy Tea Rooms (01629 810190) in Monyash. Piedaniels (01629 812687) in Bakewell serves fine French and English cuisine. There's also a pleasant cafe at Parsley Hay, 2 miles from the site.

GETTING THERE Head towards Ashbourne (from Buxton) on the A515 and, after 5 miles, take the right-hand turn signposted Hurdlow, Crowdecote and Longnor. After 400m The Royal Oak pub and campsite are on the right.

PUBLIC TRANSPORT The nearest station within walking/taxi distance is Buxton (6 miles). There's no direct bus service but the Hartington Bus goes along the A515 and will stop on the main road, ½ mile away.

OPEN All year.

THE DAMAGE Standard pitch £20 per night; super pitch £35 (with bench and firepit). 2-night minimum on weekends.

family festivals

If you love festivals, maybe your kids will
too. Spend carefree summer days with
them, dancing in a faraway field.

Podpads

Boutique
Campsite

Beach
Huts

Kids
garden

PROPER
HOG
ROAST

If you've picked up this book for research purposes, then your idea of an all-nighter has no doubt changed a bit over the years. Calpol and cocoa are probably the strongest things you want to get your hands on these days, but that doesn't mean that you have to hang up your dancing shoes altogether.

Let's face it, no one knows how to throw a party quite like we do, and the explosion of festivals across the country is colourful proof of the fact that becoming a parent – or even a grandparent – doesn't mean throwing in the party towel just yet. Of course, there are some parties that are best just left to the grown-ups. While it might not be that

appropriate to take kids to a techno-festival like Creamfields, there are plenty of family-friendly festivals that have become as essential a part of the English summer as school sports day or strawberries and cream.

These days, punters are increasingly eschewing the big commercial events, with their onsite cash machines and mobile-phone charging stations, for something a bit more handmade and authentic. Tiny boutique and family-orientated shindigs are cropping up across the UK. The festivals on the following pages are great places to take your children for a weekend of fun, whether they are babes in arms, tots, inbetweeners or sulky teens.

camp bestival

Baby sibling to Bestival on the Isle of Wight in September, Camp Bestival takes place at Lulworth Castle against the backdrop of the Jurassic Coast in Dorset. A quirky retro feel characterises this festival, which is really dominated by children. This is one for the family, and the kids' fields are fantastic, with the House of Fairy Tales, puppet shows, circus, Maypole and endless activities. There's a Dingly Dell trail, and the Breastival Mother and Baby Temple means that even the youngest family members needn't be left at home. The onsite farmer's market means that you never have to stray too far away from your comfort zone as there's good-quality food on offer, too.

Lulworth Castle, Dorset;
www.campbestival.net; July.

the larmer tree festival

Located at what was the site of a Victorian theme park, Larmer Tree is opened every year by Jools Holland and is a past winner of the Family Festival Award. It has a maximum capacity of 4,000 and there isn't a scrap of corporate sponsorship in sight, which is just as we like it. Dressing up is an essential part of the fun so children love it, and there are usually at least six stages with a thumping selection of folk, roots, blues, jazz, reggae and country music. Larmer Tree has something for everyone, with a finale on Sunday night in which festival-goers, especially kids, parade in costumes they've made over the weekend.

Larmer Tree Gardens, Nr Salisbury, Wiltshire/Dorset border;
www.larmertreefestival.co.uk; July.

shambala

Shambala is the festival expert's festival. It's maintained the sort of laid-back vibe that was what all festivals used to be like before cashpoints, photo ID and monumental barriers spoiled all the fun. A firm fixture on the summer circuit, there are few, if any, other festivals that have such a strong sense of community as this Northamptonshire stalwart. Festivals with kids can be a bit fraught, but at Shambala you almost feel you could let your toddler toddle off for a dance on their own, and some kind girl dressed as a fairy would bring him back to you (probably not wise to rely on this, though!).

Secret Country Estate, Northamptonshire;
www.shambalafestival.org; last Bank Holiday in August.

standon calling

What started as a small-scale 21st birthday party has escalated into one of the quirkiest festivals near London. But Standon Calling, set in the grounds of a riverside country manor, still retains a home-spun vibe. It's the only music festival in the UK with a swimming pool – situated next to the croquet lawn dedicated to family activities – and has an extensive kids' programme. Every year the festival is transformed by a chosen theme, from stages built like sinking pirate ships to bars in cowboys' saloons. And after the dog-show, the sock-wrestling and the face-painting is done, a fancy-dress winner is crowned on the main stage.

Standon Lordship, Ware, Hertfordshire;
www.standon-calling.com; July.

wood festival

Wood is an affirmation of life, love and family; everything that's best about a homemade festival. It's a cosy event, with a largely acoustic line-up. It defines eco-chic, with showers heated by wood-burning stoves and a solar-powered main stage (the loos are, of course, composting). There are family workshops to keep your tribe happy, as well as puppet theatres and a cycle-powered cinema and disco. The smell of woodsmoke lingers in the air and girls wear real flowers in their hair as children tumble among hay bales. There's still some of the original spirit of Woodstock at Wood... just on a very, very small scale.

Braziers Park, Oxfordshire;
www.woodfestival.com; May.

just so

Possibly the most family-friendly of the lot, Just So festival began in 2010 and has captured children's imaginations in such a way as to make Peppa Pig jealous. Set in a magical woodland in the grounds of Cheshire's Rode Hall, the festival celebrates all that is creative and ensures that every event can be attended by both parents and children. From the midnight feasts, dance workshops, campfire singing, author talks and walkabout performers, the activities and shows are inclusive and delight kids while encouraging their creativity. Thoughtful touches such as a breastfeeding tent and baby-changing areas, provide the icing on the cake.

Rode Hall, Scholar Green, Staffordshire;
www.justsofestival.org.uk; August.

lincolnshire lanes

Manor Farm, East Firsby, Market Rasen, Lincolnshire LN8 2DB 01673 878258 www.lincolnshire-lanes.com

When you've finished exploring the historic town of Lincoln, retreating through the backroads to this quiet campsite is quite a treat. By day there's acres of space, trees and nooks and crannies to explore, while by night it's a silent, sleepy escape.

This campsite has a good old-fashioned feel. It's in a peaceful, rural spot, with 20 pitches, including five in a secluded adults-only area, a couple of log cabins hidden among a grove of Christmas trees and several glamping options. There are two adjoining flat fields, surrounded by hedges, with plenty of space for games and family fun, a couple of swings and an animal area with rabbits and guinea pigs for the kids.

Situated in their own enclosure at the bottom of the second camping field are two fully equipped, comfy bell tents with real beds, duvets and pillows (bring your own bedding if you are here three nights or less). There's also a fully equipped and excellently insulated glamping pod among the trees, with a private kitchen and toilet facilities, plus that all-important hammock where you can lay back and enjoy the birdsong. A gypsy caravan finishes off the campsite's glamping offering, across a little wooden bridge and with a wide, grassy space around it.

Site owners Rosemary and Robert keep the place ship-shape and maintain its air of tranquillity by enforcing the no-noise-after-10.30pm rule. Rosemary also welcomes the log cabin dwellers with small food hampers of locally sourced produce, and Robert is an avid recycler. Please make him happy by putting aluminium, glass, plastic and paper in the right containers!

WHO'S IN Tents, campervans, caravans, family groups, dogs – yes. Same-sex groups and noisy folk – no.

ON SITE Around 20 grass pitches across 2 large, flat camping fields (15 with hook-ups if required). 2 bell tents, 2 log cabins, 1 pod and 1 gypsy caravan. 2 toilet and shower blocks, with 2 showers each and washing-up sinks (showers 20p). Disabled and baby-changing facilities, and laundry room with a washing machine and dryer.

OFF SITE It's a very easy 12-mile drive into Lincoln, home to several medieval marvels, including the Gothic cathedral (01522 561600) and the ruins of the Bishop's Palace (01522 527468). Lincoln Castle (01522 782040), encircled by medieval walls and turrets dating back to the 12th century, runs activities for children during school holidays. Entered through an imposing gateway, dotted around a long and grassy courtyard are law courts, a heritage skills centre and 2 former Victorian prisons.

FOOD & DRINK The Bottle & Glass is a traditional pub a 5-minute drive from the campsite (01673 862231), though The Inn on the Green at Ingham (01522 730354) is the best place to eat.

GETTING THERE Head north on the A15 from Lincoln. After 12 miles, take a right (Cliff Road) into Spridlington and a left onto Owmby Road. The campsite is on the left.

PUBLIC TRANSPORT Lincolnshire Council's CallConnect buses run to the site if booked in advance (Mon–Sat).

OPEN All year. Bell tents and gypsy caravan in summer only.

THE DAMAGE Camping from £12 per night; log cabins from £42 per night; gypsy caravan £45 per night; bell tents £50 per night; pod £55 per night.

watkinsons farm

Watkinsons Farm, Hall Lane, Lathom, Lancashire L40 5UG 01704 896498 www.watkinsonsfarm.co.uk

A perfect marriage of glamping comfort and a rural, off-grid setting. Do you promise to cherish and to love this campsite? In rainy times and in sunny ones? Tomorrow and always? We do!

This pastoral slice of West Lancashire is one of the oldest agricultural areas in the UK. You only have to look to the local town of Ormskirk – home to a farmer's market since medieval times – to see its bounteous produce. Vegetables, jams and homegrown goodies spill from the varied stalls, with traders capitalising on the area's convenient and accessible location.

A few miles out of town, the 120-acre expanse of Watkinsons Farm has been working the land for almost as long and has been in the hands of its current owners since the 1930s. Stretches of woodland and a patchwork of ponds dot the surroundings while vegetables are still grown in the more fertile areas. It's a perfectly picturesque scene.

It's here, backed against the woods, that Watkinsons Farm have started their newest venture – a petite bell tent glamping site, with just a pair of pre-pitched, pre-furnished beauties ideal for those looking for a quiet escape. Each tent is pitched on a flat, wooden platform, with outdoor seating and a firepit, while inside there are proper double beds, lanterns, bean bags and a box of cooking utensils with everything you could possibly need.

The all-you-need comforts go hand in hand with a traditional camping set-up. The site is completely off-grid and has a genuine camping atmosphere – think compost toilets, gas-powered showers, late-night campfires and starry nights. And for those in need of a good pillow and a sound

night's sleep, the farm is ideal. Small-scale and low-key, this is a place where you can chat to the owners rather than members of campsite staff and get first-hand recommendations on the local area.

Whether it's heading east into the hills, west to the beach or out to one of the surrounding cities, there's certainly plenty to do. A walk along the Leeds to Liverpool canal is a fantastic place to start. There are several good pubs on the waterside and the towpath has loads of space if you want to bring a bike along for a family cycle. Pedal back towards Ormskirk, meanwhile, and you can reward yourself with a cool drink and some freshly baked gingerbread. The town is apparently the birthplace of this quintessentially English biscuit, and there are plenty of bakeries where you can find the tasty treat. Naturally, more than one claims to be home of the 'very first original recipe'. You'll need your detective skills to work out who's telling the truth. And a good appetite.

WHO'S IN Glamping only. Campervans, motorhomes, caravans, tents, dogs — no.

ON SITE This is off-grid glamping: there is no mains electricity, gas or water. 2 5m bell tents are fully furnished with a double bed and bedding, bedside tables, blanket box, extra storage boxes, wood-burning stove, solid flooring, bean bag, log basket filled with logs and a cooking box. Outside there is a decking area, your own firepit with a cooking tripod, seating and a table and all the essential BBQ utensils. Compost toilets, a hot gas-powered shower and a washing-up area are all nestled in the woods. Listen for the woodpeckers, play in the field or go exploring in the woods.

OFF SITE Nearby Cedar Farm Galleries (01704 822038) is home to a café and several art galleries and independent crafts shops — well worth a visit. It's a mile to the Leeds to Liverpool Canal, where you can walk or cycle along the towpath or join a cruise. Haigh Hall and Country Park (10 miles) has 250 acres to explore, while children love Farmer Ted's Farm Park (01515 260002) and Windmill Animal Farm (01704 892282). The nearest good beaches — Southport and Formby — are within a ½-hour drive.

FOOD & DRINK There is a cooking box inside each tent with all the utensils, crockery and things you need for a BBQ. DC Scott & Sons (01695 572104) in Ormskirk is a fab local butcher, while Taylors Farm Shop (01704 895687) is located just 200m down the road. The campsite can arrange BBQ packs for breakfast, lunch or dinner. You can also take home a freshly harvested veg box from the farm. Pub-wise, the newly opened, canal-side Ring O'Bells (01704 893157), a mile from the site, is a favourite.

GETTING THERE Leave the M6 at junction 27, taking the A5209 for Ormskirk. At the 4th mini roundabout (about 5 miles) turn left onto Hall Lane. After ½ mile, turn right immediately after the sharp left-hand bend.

OPEN April–September.

THE DAMAGE £85 per night for 2 adults sharing. Plus £5 per child (3–18yrs) per stay. Under-2s stay for free.

bleasdale glamping

Brooks Farm, Bleasdale, Garstang, Lancashire PR3 1UY 01638 778325 www.lanternandlarks.co.uk

Fabulously fitting for a big rural estate: posh glamping luxuries and acres of private countryside just for you. And, best of all, the chance to enjoy one of England's greatest hidden treasures.

The Forest of Bowland is a shamefully undiscovered place. It's understandable, of course, given its neighbours – the Peak District to the south, the Yorkshire Dales in the east and Cumbria's Lake District to the north. Hemmed between motorways, though, the Forest of Bowland beats them all hands-down for accessibility. And once you leave the tarmac it quickly becomes apparent that the area is no slouch when it comes to scenery either. Bleasdale is a perfect case in point. A good half-mile of private driveway leads you away from the backwater B-road you took from the M6. The vast country estate is fronted by old workmen's cottages, perched at the entrance to the grounds that date back several centuries. In the background flanks of dark, crowded trees give way to gently rising ridges, climbing up to Fair Snape Fell – one of the largest hills in the Forest of Bowland – before curling round a crescent-shaped valley to Parlick Pike. It's a classic British landscape, and difficult to beat, no matter where you go.

The site itself is of the high-end glamping variety. This is a place where, regardless of how muddy you get stalking wildlife or splashing about in the river, you can return to the utmost of canvas comforts. Five spacious, well-furnished safari tents are pitched with their backs to a strip of den-friendly woodland, overlooking a private section of the languid River Brock. Inside they're divided into three separate bedrooms and a large open-plan living area with a kitchen in the corner. A central wood-burning stove adds to the cosy feel, accompanied by furnishings that wouldn't look out of place in the elegant outhouses of the estate. Attached to the back is a private bathroom and toilet with a piping hot gas-powered shower and thoughtfully provided toiletries in cute miniature bottles.

It's a place where you can hide away from the clamour of daily life, amid tranquil surroundings that provide a large dose of calm and relaxation. The campsite has immediate access to several fantastic local trails and, if you head from the riverbanks in the direction of Parlick Pike, a heather-topped cone of a hill, there's a Stone Age circle around ten minutes' walk away. Most days you'll be the only one here, so you can stand around holding hands and praying to the ancient fire gods. When you get back to camp, check if it's worked by laying out the campfire and then praying to the god of marshmallows… or just buying them from Bleasdale's honesty shop.

WHO'S IN Glamping only, so no tents, campervans or caravans. Dogs, families, large groups, couples – yes.

ON SITE 5 safari-style tents spread at intervals around a large field. Tents sleep up to 6 people in 3 separate rooms – 1 double, 1 twin and a bunk bed (bedding and linen provided). The tents are furnished throughout with everything you could possibly need, with sofas, dining furniture, a wood-burning stove, a kitchen with gas hobs and cooking utensils, plus an in-tent bathroom with a shower and toilet.

OFF SITE The main attraction of the Forest of Bowland is the space to explore on foot or by bike, with an excellent cycle network and plenty of footpaths. For something different, Cobble Hey Farm & Gardens (01995 602643), a working farm and gardens a few miles away, is worth a visit, though this might be a little upstaged by the Bowland Wild Boar Park (01995 61554), a popular spot where you can meet squealing wild boar piglets. There's plenty of other wildlife here, too, including deer, llamas and goats.

FOOD & DRINK You can organise extras when you make your booking: breakfast hampers, BBQ packs and the like are all available. As for pubs, there's The Tillotsons Arms in nearby Chipping (01995 61568), which does food, or the much fancier and better-known Inn at Whitewell (01200 448222).

GETTING THERE Leave the M6 at junction 32 and take the A6 north towards Garstang. After 4½ miles turn right just before the Shell garage, following the signs for Beacon Fell Country Park. Go over the canal, railway and motorway. Fork right and take the next left (signed Chipping) and continue for 2½ miles to the T-junction. Turn left. After 300m turn right (signposted Bleasdale). Continue for 2 miles and turn left at the lodge with a 'private drive' sign. Take the first sharp turn to your right. Brooks Farm is on the left and the site is signposted up the hill.

OPEN March–October.

THE DAMAGE From £395–£455 for a 3-night break. See the website for more details.

catgill campsite

Bolton Abbey, North Yorkshire BD23 6HA 01756 710247 www.catgillcampsite.co.uk

The lumps and bumps of this rolling camping meadow are all a part of its charm. This is real Yorkshire farmland, and with so much space, marvellous Bolton Abbey on the doorstep and Hesketh Farm Park around the corner, the kids certainly won't complain.

Set in the surrounding estate of Bolton Abbey, Catgill Campsite is a gloriously green meadow space that perfectly mixes the old with the new. Less than a mile along the Wharfe Valley, the campsite snuggles among the grass in picturesque splendour: campfire smoke wafts through the air with the same lazy ease as the river that runs alongside, and children run in the open space beyond the tents. It's a charmingly timeless scene.

In total there are around 30 grassy pitches, each offering spectacular views across the lush open landscape, dotted with sheep and criss-crossed by dry stone walls. A newly built sanitary block sits in the centre of the site, a tiny shop selling essentials has been recently added and plans for a small playground are afoot. Most kids, though, love tracing the small stream that trickles through the field to the River Wharfe. It heads via the ruins of the abbey or, to be correct, Bolton Priory, the real name of the ruined Augustinian monastery, founded in 1154.

After stopping amid the stone walls to admire the Gothic architecture or attend one of the services (which still run to this day) you can wander down to the riverside picnic area or beyond to Bolton Abbey village. This delightful little settlement is well tucked away among the greens and browns of the landscape and boasts a couple of restaurants and tea rooms despite its modest size. While it's a worthy place to enjoy some traditional grub, children and adults alike should continue to the village railway station – a preserved, volunteer-run line that plays host to some magnificent steam trains, including everyone's favourite, Thomas the Tank Engine.

For most, however, the draw of this campsite is its access to miles upon miles of all-weather walking routes on its doorstep. The tents-only policy makes it perfect for those on the hoof looking for fellow backpackers, or cyclists on the quiet country lanes hoping to avoid the caravan crowd; and, if the local paths aren't enough for you, a short trip north leaves you smack-bang in the middle of the Yorkshire Dales National Park, renowned for its outstanding scenery and diverse wildlife. Don't scamper off into the hills too quickly, though. The real gateway to the Dales is via the lively nearby market town of Skipton, home to a castle dating back to 1090 and Yorkshire's finest fish and chips at Bizzie Lizzies. It seems that, with so much to do, you could be at Catgill for a while!

Welcome to **Catgill Campsite**

WHO'S IN Tents only. Families, groups and dogs – yes. Single-sex groups – no.

ON SITE 50 spacious tent spots and a large grassy area on site for kids to play. A new wash-block with showers, wash basins and toilets including a dedicated disabled/family room in both male and female washrooms. Plugs for hairdryers, straighteners and razors. There's also a separate washing-up room with 6 sinks and 2 fridge/freezers.

OFF SITE Bolton Abbey (01756 718009) is just under a mile's walk away to the east and is free to enter (though £7 to park). Embsay & Bolton Abbey Steam Railway (01756 710614) is a similar distance to the south. Hesketh Farm Park (01756 710444), around the corner, is a pleasant family attraction, a working sheep and beef farm with animals to feed and stroke, tractor tours and a straw maze.

FOOD & DRINK There's a tiny onsite shop selling essentials, and a few pubs and restaurants close at hand, including the 350-year-old Devonshire Arms (01756 710441), with a good brasserie and a Michelin-starred restaurant. But it's tea rooms that are the staple here: Bolton Abbey Tea Cottage (01756 718000) serves morning coffee, lunch and afternoon tea from its splendid position overlooking the priory ruins and the river; the Victorian-built Cavendish Pavillion (01756 710245) does hot and cold food throughout the day, while Blueberry Kitchen (01756 718000), in the village, offers soups, sandwiches and cakes. The 1950s-style Yorkshire Ice Cream Parlour (01756 710685) serves tasty homemade ice cream that kids will love.

GETTING THERE Follow the A59 towards Bolton Abbey and, at the Bolton Abbey roundabout, exit towards the village. Turn left in the centre of the village and, after ¾ mile, the campsite is on the right.

PUBLIC TRANSPORT The Pride of the Dales bus 74 runs between Ilkley and Grassington every 2 hours and goes through Bolton Abbey village. Both towns have train stations.

OPEN Late March–early October.

THE DAMAGE Adults £10 a night (£12 bank holidays); children (3–15yrs) £5 a night (£7 bank holidays); under-3s free.

masons campsite

Ainhams House, Appletreewick, Skipton, North Yorkshire BD23 6DD 01756 720275 www.masonscampsite.co.uk

What a treat! A campsite that's actually run by campers who know all about choosing a great site. The river provides plenty of opportunity for fishing and you can make a dramatic river-entry via a rope swing, handily located on the bank.

Situated in the heart of the Yorkshire Dales, by the banks of the River Wharfe, Masons is so good that even the owners still camp here. When their favourite campsite in the Yorkshire Dales came up for sale, Georgie and Grant bought Masons and set about scrubbing up an already popular site. Today it's about as good as camping gets.

You no longer have to walk a mile to the nearest shop, since their onsite 1968 Airstream office sells essential food and camping items, while the Coffee & Bread Shed serves coffee, fresh croissants, baguettes and more. There is heaps of space to pitch in the two main fields, plus a handful of yurts, safari tents, and a couple of classic VW campervans to hire. The flat camping fields have plenty of space for kite-flying and ball games, and lots of families bring lilos and dinghies to frolic in the river. Both fields are backed by the wide and mainly shallow Wharfe where you can try your hand at fly-fishing from the large flat stones while the kids happily pass the time paddling around and jumping in and out of the water. The resident chickens and ducks are popular with younger children, too, while footpaths lead from the site along the river to Burnsall, a popular picnicking and swimming spot. Appletreewick and Barden Bridge are also just a short jaunt away, both with excellent family-friendly country pubs housed in typical old Yorkshire-stone buildings.

WHO'S IN Tents, campervans, caravans, dogs – yes.

ON SITE 2 camping meadows, 6 yurts, 2 safari tents and 2 VW campervans. The first field has 40 pitches with electricity and in the second field (weekends only) tents pitch along the riverbank, leaving plenty of space for ball games. 8 washing-up sinks, 10 showers (including a family/disabled room) and 10 toilets and 10 handbasins each (male/female). A well-stocked shop sells bacon, eggs, milk, sweets, toys, food and camping essentials. Their Coffee & Bread Shed sells hot drinks, fresh bread and pastries.

OFF SITE Footpaths run from the site to Burnsall, which is a popular picnicking and swimming spot, as well as to Appletreewick and Barden Bridge. Bolton Abbey and the Embsay & Bolton Abbey Steam Railway (01756 710614) are just up the road. Billy Bob's Play Barn (01756 711826) and Hesketh Farm Park (01756 710444) are a 20-minute drive.

FOOD & DRINK The New Inn (01751 720252) has a selection of quirky beers, while the 16th-century Craven Arms (01756 720270) has log fires, gas lamps and stone-flagged floors, and is the shortest of strolls away. Both serve food.

GETTING THERE Turn north off the A59 between Skipton and Harrogate, onto the B6160 at Bolton Abbey. After 3 miles take the first right after Barden Tower, signposted Appletreewick, and continue for 2 miles; turn left at the T-junction into Appletreewick and the site is at the foot of the hill.

PUBLIC TRANSPORT Dales buses run between Ilkley and Grassington through Appletreewick.

OPEN Mid March–end October.

THE DAMAGE Pitches from £20 including one car. Dogs £1. Glamping options from £69 a night.

crow's nest

Gristhorpe, Filey, North Yorkshire YO14 9PS 01723 582206 www.crowsnestcaravanpark.com

Swimming pool, games room, playground... there's no denying the family-friendly functionality of this clifftop campsite but it's the location by Gristhorpe Bay and the tumbling footpath down to the beach that make it a real winner.

Crow's Nest is a tale of two campsites. The first is a large holiday park with a bar, café, fish and chip shop, indoor swimming pool and row upon row of static caravans. Not exactly *Cool Camping*. But venture a little further and you'll find a large tents-only field with panoramic views over the sea and across the Yorkshire Wolds and Vale of Pickering. A children's playground forms a handy boundary between these two very different areas.

The tent field climbs up and then slopes gently down towards the clifftop. There's room for 150–200 tents (and the odd campervan) on a pitch-where-you-like basis. As you head up the hill, you'll spy some secluded areas surrounded by hedges for small groups of tents, and the closer you get to the sea, the quieter and more peaceful the site becomes. Large family groups head for the serviced pitches near the playground, while a mixture of couples, groups and families are spread across the rest of the site. The adventurous and sure of foot can take the path down the cliffs to the shingle beach at Gristhorpe Bay and, if you're lucky, you might spot members of the local seal colony that live on and around the rocks here.

WHO'S IN Tents, 1 or 2 campervans, dogs, groups – yes.

ON SITE Crow's Nest has a large tent field that accepts around 150 tents without electric hook-up. There are also 20 tent pitches with electric hook-ups (plus 50 touring caravan pitches and 220 static caravans). An award-winning ablutions block sits on the edge of the camping field, featuring ladies and gents facilities, family shower rooms, a disabled shower room, pot wash and laundry. There's a well-stocked shop along with other facilities in the main holiday park. No campfires.

OFF SITE The North Yorkshire Coast boasts a multitude of great days out. The Cleveland Way runs along the clifftop in front of the site and takes you into Filey (around 2½ miles) in one direction and Scarborough (5 miles) in the other.

FOOD & DRINK The Copper Horse (01723 862029) restaurant in Seamer has a theatrical theme and award-winning food. For great fish and chips there is a takeaway in the park. Or head to Inghams (01723 513320) on Belle Vue Street in Filey.

GETTING THERE The site is just off the A165 between Scarborough and Filey. A couple of miles north of Filey there's a roundabout with a petrol station on the corner. Turn here, then carry on along the road. Crow's Nest is the second caravan park on the left.

PUBLIC TRANSPORT The nearest station is Filey, but most trains run to Scarborough. Bus 120 runs between Scarborough and Bridlington and stops at the bottom of the lane.

OPEN March–October.

THE DAMAGE Tents (up to 4 people) £22–£32 per night.

fisherground campsite

Fellside Cottage, Eskdale, Holmrook, Cumbria CA19 1TF 01946 723349 www.fishergroundcampsite.co.uk

Marshmallow-toasting? Check. Water? Check. Playgrounds? Check. Trains? Check – all the the things that make camping really cool for kids. And you can even arrive at the site's own station by steam locomotive.

This is a great site for kids. It ticks all their campsite boxes and probably a few more besides. Campfires are not only allowed but positively encouraged in selected areas, with bags of logs complete with kindling and firelighters sold onsite each evening. Owner Mike takes a 'we like you to succeed' approach – just don't forget to pack the marshmallows.

The first thing that meets you on arrival is the pond, fed by a stream and usually full of children playing on tyre rafts – it makes a perfect focal point where kids can get to know each other. The playground has everything your young adventurers desire in the way of zip-wires, climbing frames, tyre rope-swings and outdoors courses. And there's an added extra: the site sits along the route of the Ravenglass and Eskdale steam railway line – a fab way to arrive if you're coming by public transport. So if you've walked into the nearby hamlet of Boot and there are some tired little legs as a result, hop on board for a scenic choo-choo trip back to camp. For the adults, the site is in the heart of the Eskdale Valley, a relatively quiet part of the Lake District, far from its most challenging hustle and bustle. Rugged, bracken-clad fells, woods and grazing sheep provide a splendid backdrop to rest your eyes on when you do eventually find time to relax.

WHO'S IN Tents, campervans, dogs – yes. Caravans – no.

ON SITE Unmarked pitches in 2 main areas: a large field near to the children's playground and a smaller, quieter field near to the wash-block, with wheel rims for campfires. The wash-block has ample hand basins, showers (50p) and loos. There is a washing machine, 3 tumble dryers, a boot-dryer and freezer. The kids will be straight into the pond before you've had a chance to even pitch your tent. There are rocks and trees for climbing on and plenty of space for ball games. No shop on site, but you can buy logs, kindling and firelighters. No noise after 10.30pm.

OFF SITE Go by steam train to Ravenglass, or make the short trip to Dalegarth. From here you can walk into Boot or up to Stanley Force, following the tumbling beck up to the waterfall. A short walk towards Eskdale Green takes you along the River Esk, where a shallow area by the bridge is a good spot for a quick (if chilly) dip.

GETTING THERE Follow the A5092 towards Broughton-in-Furness, turning off at a set of traffic lights towards Ulpha. Head into Ulpha and turn left up the steep hill signed 'Eskdale'. Follow the road to the King George IV pub and turn right to Boot. Fisherground campsite is 300m on the left.

PUBLIC TRANSPORT The 618 bus from Ambleside and Windermere stops at Fell Foot around 5 times a day.

OPEN Early March–late October.

THE DAMAGE Adults £7, children (3–15yrs) £3.50, vehicles £2.50, dogs £1.50 per night. During school holidays there's a surcharge of £7 per night for tents with 6 berths and more and £5 per night for tents with 3 berths and more.

the quiet site

Ullswater, Penrith, Cumbria CA11 0LS 07768 727016 www.thequietsite.co.uk

While the Quiet Site aims to please everyone, there's a huge family focus here, with an adventure playground and a games room inside what is surely the world's best campsite pub. It may bring out the inner child of a few grown-ups in the group.

Despite its unusual name, the reality is that The Quiet Site isn't much quieter than your average campsite. But the name is enough to put off any rowdies or big groups, so it's certainly quieter than some of the more boisterous Lake District options.

Standing atop the fells above what many believe is the region's finest stretch of water, The Quiet Site is a peaceful escape from nearby Glenridding and a sanctuary of calm from the Lakeland summer crowds. It's also ideal for accessing the best Lakeland footpaths. On arrival you'll get a handcrafted walking guide with decent walks around the area, tailored to all family members and interests, from full-on near-vertical workouts to ambles with the kids. You can also get a watery perspective of Ullswater from the famous Ullswater Steamer or from a rowing or motor boat, both easily hired at Watermillock or Glenridding marina. Come the end of the day, you don't even have to make much effort to enjoy a well-earned pint. The Quiet Site has its own cosy pub, simply named 'The Pub', housed in the farm's original stone barn – though sadly they don't serve food... then you'd never have to leave!

If you're looking for serenity, great walking or just want to kick back with the family, The Quiet Site delivers on all three counts. But be warned that it already has a hardcore following. Best keep it all a little hush-hush...

WHO'S IN Tents, glampers, caravans, campervans, dogs – yes. Large groups (unless pre-arranged) – no.

ON SITE As well as traditional camping there are 15 pods, 5 bell tents and 6 hobbit holes – cosy, family-sized, grass-roofed pods carved out of the hillside. There's an excellent and cosy onsite pub in a converted barn, with table tennis for kids, and a wash-block with hot showers and a washing-up area. There's also a small shop with all the basics. The Quiet Site is committed to sustainable tourism with all hot water and heating is provided using renewable sources.

OFF SITE A print-out with the best local walking routes and attractions is provided on arrival. Catch the Ullswater Steamer from Glenridding to Pooley Bridge (01768 482229) or indeed just enjoy the cruise around the lake. History bods may want to explore nearby Dalemain House (01768 486450).

FOOD & DRINK On the shores of Lake Ullswater, The Sharrow Bay Hotel (01768 486301) has a Michelin-starred restaurant. You can enjoy lunch or dinner there but they're most famous for their afternoon teas. The site's onsite pub serves a variety of local ales but no food - for that you should head to the Brackenrigg Inn (01768 486206), overlooking Ullswater.

GETTING THERE Follow the A66 to Keswick and then take the A592 toward Glenridding, turning right at the Brackenrigg Inn. The site is 1¼ miles up here on your right.

OPEN All year.

THE DAMAGE Pitches £12–£27 a night, including 1 tent, 1 car and 2 adults. Extra adults £3, children (5–15yrs) £2 and under-4s free. Dogs £1 per night. Hobbit holes £55–£80 per night for 2 adults and up to 4 children.

kestrel lodge camping

Bassenthwaite, Keswick, Cumbria CA12 4QX 017687 76752 www.kestrellodge.co.uk

At the end of a good day's walk, you'll find yourself washing mud off your boots, mud off the dog and mud off the kids. All the hallmarks of a good day out in the Lakes. And a sign that this live-and-let-live campsite is well prepped for family campers.

Louise Smith and Andrea Bramhall seem to have found a winning formula – find an old farm in the most enviable location you can think of, give it a good makeover with a lawn-mower, a few signposts and a brand spanking new block of modern showers, then open up the gates and let the campers roll in! Their first campsite, in North Norfolk – which they took over almost 10 years ago – received a solid thumbs-up from all the *Cool Camping* clan, and we very much expect it to be exactly the same at Kestrel Lodge.

Set in the shadow of mighty Skiddaw and a stone's throw from sparkling Bassenthwaite Lake to the south-west, Kestrel Lodge Camping is a traditional Lakeland campsite on an 18th-century farm. Grassy pitches enjoy stonking vistas across to the hills, while a clutch of electric hook-ups means

a few campervans are welcome, too, so expect to see the odd VW camper chugging up the lane.

Louise, Andrea and their family are personable and friendly and seem to be just as in awe of the surroundings as most of their guests. They can point you in the direction of each of the nine Wainwright walks you can do from the campsite, as well show you the route to the nearest pub. It's with fond memories that they remember their younger days camping here and it's clear they want to explore the surroundings of their new home as much as every visitor. You almost feel guilty trekking off into the hills without them. The ethos, they tell us, is "small, quiet, friendly, traditional, but with nice hot showers, and somewhere to clean your boots and dogs". We couldn't agree more.

JACKA

WHO'S IN Tents, campervans, dogs, families, scouts, DofE groups – yes. Larger groups and single-sex groups should get in touch first.

ON SITE 30 grass pitches, electrical hook-ups available. Newly refurbished toilet and shower block, covered cooking area, laundry facilities, a freezer for ice packs, a small shop selling all the basics and Wi-Fi available. Campfires are allowed in the firepits provided. There's a small flock of free-range chickens and ducks and a super-friendly Shetland pony called Mo. The Cumbrian Way footpath runs alongside the campsite.

OFF SITE Skiddaw looms on the horizon and therefore gets all the glory, but there are 9 other mighty mountains that can be tackled from the campsite. It's around 5 miles to the summit of the fabulously named Great Cockup and a 7-mile walk up Binsey – Louise and Andrea can help you plan family-friendly routes if needed. It's 6 miles to Keswick and 7 to Cockermouth, both full of excellent eateries, shops and museums that all prove there's more to the Lakes than just walking. Derwent Pencil Museum (017687 73626) in Keswick, Honister Slate Mine (017687 77230) and Wordsworth House and Gardens (01900 824805) are all good examples.

FOOD & DRINK There's a great pub in Bassenthwaite village, The Sun Inn (017687 76439), a pleasant 20-minute walk away, serving comforting pub food and with real ales on tap.

GETTING THERE Leave the A591 at Bassenthwaite and follow the road out of the village alongside the river; ½ mile out of the village you will see a sign on the left for 'Kestrel Lodge Camping'.

PUBLIC TRANSPORT There is a regular bus service from Workington to Penrith (both with train stations) that passes along the A591 and stops outside Bassenthwaite church, just over a mile from the campsite.

OPEN March–November.

THE DAMAGE £7–£9 per adult, £3.50–£4.50 per child (3–16yrs). 2-night minimum on weekends, and 3-night minimum on bank holidays and Easter. Under-3s and dogs stay free.

balloch o' dee

Kirkcowan, Newton Stewart, Wigtownshire DG8 0ET 01671 830708 www.ballochodee.com

With horses for neighbours and chickens for playmates, Balloch O' Dee campsite is the perfect place for countryside-loving families in need of space and stargazing – all part of a back-to-basics camping experience.

Balloch O' Dee's farm campsite is located in one of the Lowlands' most stunning areas – right on the edge of fir-cloaked Galloway Forest Park. With fantastically clear night skies, it's the only European designated Dark Skies forest. James and Hazel bought the place in 2010 and, just 12 months later, opened its gates to campers in search of a rural retreat. Their hard work has paid off as the campsite is fast becoming a family favourite. Back when we first visited in those early days it was the stark rusticity of the place, tucked amid inspiring landscapes and boasting ancient stone farm buildings, that made it really stand out. Years later, with the addition of electricity, toilet and showers, there have certainly been changes, yet the subtlety with which James and Hazel have shaped the campsite means that the same unpretentious, rural camping character still shines through.

There is plenty of space and the large camping field offers spectacular views across the surrounding countryside. The atmosphere is relaxed and informal; kids can often be found paddling or trying to catch crayfish in the farm's tinkling burn before dragonflies appear at dusk. Communal campfires accompanied by evening sing-songs are commonplace while, in the morning, campers are woken by the dawn chorus and get to throw open their tent doors to the sight of Culvennan Fell, framed by the morning mist…

The aforementioned stone buildings have been tastefully converted to a surprisingly cosy sanitary block. Large 'rainfall' showers provide the perfect way to warm up if bad weather catches you out on a fell walk, while thoughtful touches like free handmade soaps and scented candles show the owners care as much for the site and their guests now as they did when they first unlatched the gates all those years ago. The same thoughtfulness can be seen in their newest additions – a bunk-house bothy, located in the old cowshed, and the wooden roundhouse at the bottom of the field, each with fire-fed range ovens and an unbeatably snug interior, plus a Mongolian yurt, new for 2015 and complete with a wood-burning stove.

Adjacent to the campsite is Balloch O' Dee's trekking centre, which offers a warm welcome to young horseriders. Tuition is available, or you can simply enjoy a free ride around the site or help Hazel with the grooming. By day, little ones have a great view on horseback across the surrounding countryside. By night, they can keep their eyes peeled for shooting stars and ponder what sort of fun other campers might be having in another galaxy, far, far away.

WHO'S IN Tents, campervans, caravans, dogs (on a lead), well-behaved groups – yes.

ON SITE 30–40 pitches for tents with some hook-ups. Bothy (sleeps 5–7), roundhouse (sleeps 5–7) and Mongolian yurt (sleeps 4–6). A converted barn serves as a shower and washing-up area and the toilets are probably the best we've seen. Stone-built BBQs dotted around. Dozens of rare-breed hens roam around the site and the challenge is to find and collect their eggs each morning for a hearty omelette. Campfires are permitted in previously used spots.

OFF SITE The pony-trekking centre should provide hours of fun for budding jockeys. Children are welcome to stay at the stables for the day and groom the horses, learn more about their new four-legged friends and join in with the mucking out (bring wellies and waterproofs!). Three Lochs Holiday Park (01671 830304) is a couple of miles down the road. Activities on offer range from archery to mountain biking. You can book fishing at Loch Heron and Loch Ronald at the park's reception to go after pike as large as 30lbs for supper.

FOOD & DRINK Check out the House o' Hill Hotel at Glentrool (01671 840243), which has a fabulous location at the edge of Gallery Forest and a menu to match – crammed full of local produce and with something tasty for even the youngest of diners; try the homemade fishcakes.

GETTING THERE Leave the M6, signposted for Stranraer (A75), and continue westward, past Newton Stewart and on for a further 6 miles. Here you'll see a right-turn for 'The Three Lochs'. The campsite is 1½ miles along this road, on the right.

OPEN All year (Mongolian yurt June–October only).

THE DAMAGE Regular pitch £15 per night, electric pitch £20 per night. Glamping from £50 per night. Dogs free.

comrie croft

Braincroft, Crieff, Perthshire PH7 4JZ 01764 670140 www.comriecroft.com

Adventure-loving families scramble, run and jump this way... Comrie Croft has forest to roam around, mountain-bike trails to race along and a small loch in which to fish. Truly embrace the great outdoors from the moment you pitch your tent.

Before the Act of Union, many Scots lived on crofts, smallholdings of land where communal living was the norm. In the heart of deepest Perthshire, this communal, everyone-in-it-together ethic has been re-created at Comrie Croft. Run by a co-operative of like-minded, environmentally aware individuals, this is no mere campsite. Yes, they take tents, but they've also got Nordic katas, an onsite Tea Garden and a superb bike shop, the latter handy for exploring the network of trails that snake off up the Croft's wooded hillside. First-timers might feel most secure down in the main camping field near all the facilities, but more adventurous souls will want to push on up into the forest, where secluded pitches await, each with its own campfire. Four of the seven katas lie up here, too; they're a sort of Swedish tipi complete with a wood-burning stove and a large sleeping area strewn with animal skins.

There is little need to leave the Croft. Down by the carpark is a superb camp store stocking everything from fluorescent camping pegs to free-range eggs and fresh local meat. Up the hill are those trails. You can walk them, but biking provides a much better way of exploring more of the hillside. On a busy day – and most weekends are busy – Comrie Croft buzzes with life, just as crofts once did all over this charmingly scenic corner of highland Perthshire.

WHO'S IN Tents, dogs, groups – yes. Caravans, campervans – no.
ON SITE 42 camping pitches. 7 katas. Campfires allowed. Solar- and wind-powered amenities block with toilets, showers, family and disabled facilities. Compost loos in the upper meadow. Excellent camping store. Blue and red mountain-bike trails and skills park with bike hire and helmets available. Network of marked walking trails and picnic areas.
OFF SITE The high land beyond the boundaries of the Croft is tough going but opens up sweeping views of Strathearn for well-equipped hikers. Perthshire is excellent both for walking and hiking; a map detailing local routes is posted and available for sale in the store. The Croft lies between the characterful Highland Perthshire towns of Crieff and Comrie. The Auchingarrich Wildlife Park (01764 679469) is a handy family attraction just south of Comrie.
FOOD & DRINK The onsite Tea Garden (Easter–end of Oct) is ideal for breakfast and lunch. Comrie offers a reasonable chippie (07514 678833) and the Royal Hotel (01764 679200), with a hunting lodge-style bar and restaurant.
GETTING THERE The campsite is 2 miles out of Comrie on the Crieff road heading east, signposted on the left.
PUBLIC TRANSPORT The Stagecoach no.15 bus runs from Perth to St Fillans, stopping at the end of the campsite road. Sadly, a recent change in the bus service provider, means bicycles are no longer permitted onboard.
OPEN All year.
THE DAMAGE Adults £8–£10 a night, children (5–18yrs) £4–£5, under-5s free. Katas £229 per weekend (Fri–Sun), £99 per weeknight. 10% off for car-free guests.

ecocamp glenshee

Blacklunans, Blairgowrie, Perthshire PH10 7LA 01250 882284 www.ecocampglenshee.co.uk

Only Scotland does starry nights like this and in this unspoiled patch of Perthshire you can kick back and take it all in. If your kids need space to let off steam and silence to sleep soundly, then you may as well book now.

The owners' suggestion that you bring a torch with you to the Ecocamp Glenshee carpark is a good indication of what lies ahead. This is not a town-side campsite with corridors of well-lit tarmac and enough caravans to house a small army. Instead, Glenshee opens up before you into a gargantuan grassy space that, at night, is bathed beneath a sea of twinkling stars that only rural Scotland can boast the likes of.

Having popped your head into the home of welcoming owners Fiona and Simon to say hello and check in, you can fully survey the scene before you. To one side a stone bothy awaits any items you don't want in your tent – inside there is a fridge-freezer, a sink with hot water, all the cooking utensils you need and space to securely store your bikes – while, beyond, the campsite is peppered with the varied colours of pre-pitched accommodation.

In the bottom of the glen sit a pair of green shepherd's huts, at the far end there's a collection of pods and, in between, there's a hilltop family tent with smoke wafting from its chimney. Two more colourful bell tents, striped in purple and blue, are also set amid mown patches of grass. Together it sounds like an awful lot of options, yet they are all set so widely apart that the field still offers acres of open space in between. Children run about by day and at night campfires crackle outside every

structure, the starlight picking out the hills that create the valley walls.

It's no accident that there's so much space. These things aren't unintentional. All that extra breathing room has allowed Simon and Fiona to plant young trees – a small part of their eco-friendly ethos that spreads across the site. Along with locally sourced building materials, solar-powered lighting and a good recycling policy, the eco-attitude also reaps the benefit of excellent food for campers, with eggs fresh from the campsite chickens and meat from surrounding farms that are sure to fuel you up for an outdoor day ahead.

You needn't wate too much petrol to enjoy the surroundings either. From the campsite you can enjoy trekking with Simon and Fiona's llamas or take a map and follow one of their well-organised geo-caching (outdoor treasure-hunting) routes. Right on the edge of the Cairngorms National Park, it's a well-located spot for hopping straight onto nearby footpaths and also boasts heaps of outdoor activities in the vicinity. Hiking and mountain-biking are particularly popular, with some of the UK's most challenging trails on offer to those with two wheels. When you return you are guaranteed the warmth of a hot shower and the cosy bothy to relax in too. It's the simple pleasures that make it so worthwhile.

WHO'S IN Glampers, campers, tents, small campervans, dogs, couples, families, groups and exclusive hire – yes. Caravans and motorhomes – no.

ON SITE 10 tent pitches (2 suitable for small campervans), 6 wooden pods, 4 bell tents, 2 shepherd's huts and a goods wagon. 5 showers and 5 toilets; all showers are free and have instant hot water at any time of the day. There are family showers and separate facilities. There is a communal area – 'the bothy' – for cooking and washing-up, with food storage, cutlery, crockery, pots and pans, fridge, free tea and coffee, clothes-drying and a wood-burning stove. Onsite fun includes geo-caching, llama trekking and feeding the animals – hens, goats, donkeys and llamas – along with archery, sea-kayaking and more, run by Outdoor Explore, who will come and collect you from the site.

OFF SITE There's a billboard at the campsite that picks out many of the best local attractions – gardens, castles, the nearest distillery – with the local villages of Pitlochry and Braemar, the best spots for a good mooch around. There's an activity centre, The Blackwater Outdoor Centre (01738 472236) 2 miles away and the 103-mile-long Cateran Trail runs nearby, taking in the best of the local countryside.

FOOD & DRINK There is a small but excellent village shop located 5 miles away in Kirkton of Glenisla, which is also home to an atmospheric old coaching inn – Glenisla Hotel (01575 582223).

GETTING THERE The campsite is 1 mile off the A93. Take the turning signposted for Blacklunans and head through the village, following the campsite signs.

OPEN All year.

THE DAMAGE Tents from £10 per person per night. Glamping accommodation £60–£140 a night.

greenhillock glamping

Lower Greenhillock, Kirkbuddo, Forfar, Angus DD8 2NL 07538 819058 www.greenglamping.co.uk

There's a reason it's not called Greyhillock. Wild grasses grow, dragonflies dance around the lily pond and birds flitter in the trees. It's all green here, and there are plenty of bug-hunting, pond-dipping and den-building activities to make the most of it.

If the point of camping is to immerse yourself in nature, few places help you do it better than Greenhillock Glamping. A five-acre site with just 25 pitches and a scattering of beautiful bell tents, it exudes a wonderfully wild and natural aura, yet without simply abandoning you in the wilderness. In fact, Greenhillock is really a proper family site – a haven for kids, and very well-equipped with showers, toilets, communal cooking and even a chillout area. Its sense of nature comes not from feeling isolated in the wilds, but rather from being a part of the natural surroundings. The pitches are generous and well-spaced and the communal field kitchen is perfect if the weather doesn't play ball. There's an 'Art Shack' for creative kids, while those seeking comfort can ditch their tent and plump for one of the five bell tents instead – fully furnished with beds, wooden floors and a private deck area with firepit.

As a place to explore, though, Greenhillock really is something else. Nature trails, some mown narrowly among the long wild grasses, others meandering into surrounding copse, weave and separate through the surroundings, linking back up again like a vast natural maze. Hedgerows and mature trees provide enough fallen branches to set the scene for the next World Den-Building Championships, and a pond in a quiet corner of the site is set up with wooden-board platforms around its edges – purpose-built spots from which you can poke and prod with a net and bucket; insect inspecting is an essential part of any stay here. The owners even provide some basic scientific equipment to help you out.

The abundance of nature here – thanks to more than 20 years of careful cultivation – also make it an excellent spot for walking and cycling, with quiet B roads keeping things safe and sound. More hardy types, though, should hop in the car and head north to the Cairngorms National Park, where formidable mountains offer tougher outdoor trails. The east coast is a similar distance in the opposite direction and a good alternative place to end the day, munching fish and chips along the harbour at Arbroath. If you are not whiling away the hours around the campfire, that is – which is the essential end-of-the-day therapy for most visitors at Greenhillock Glamping.

Tents, dogs, large groups (by prior arrangement) – yes. Caravans, campervans and motorhomes – no.

ON SITE 25 pitches and 5 furnished bell tents (sleeping 4), with wooden floors, a private deck and firepit. The site is car-free, with parking in an adjacent plot. Campfires permitted. 5 compost toilets, 3 solar-powered showers. Field Kitchen (communal cooking and chillout area), Art Shack (covered space with arts materials) and a Bug Zone (space for kids to examine mini beasts and pond critters). Regular nature walks, pond-dipping, den-building, bug-hunting and more.

OFF SITE The site is equidistant from the mountains of the Cairngorms National Park and the dynamic geography of the east coast. It's around a half-hour drive to the national park, 20 minutes or so to the coast. Try heading straight for Arbroath – a medieval port that's now the heart of the Scottish fishing industry. Sampling the fresh seafood is a must. Visit grand Arbroath Abbey (01241 878756), founded in 1178 by King William the Lion, or pop in to see Kerr's Miniature Railway (01241 874074), the oldest in Scotland. In the opposite direction, 14th-century Glamis Castle (01307 840393) – the late Queen Mother's childhood home – is 15 minutes by car.

FOOD & DRINK Communal BBQs are provided. BBQ packs and other local produce can be supplied by prior arrangement. The owners are also building a pizza oven and stock the produce so you can make your own. Away from the site, it's a cycle or short drive south to The Wellbank Inn (01382 350922) and Craigton Coach Inn (01382 370223). For seafood near Arbroath, try But 'n Ben (01241 877223).

GETTING THERE From Whigstreet and the A90, follow the B9127 for 4 miles; cross the railway bridge and, where the road turns sharply right, take the farm track on the left, signed Greenhillock.

OPEN Mid April–mid September.

THE DAMAGE Pitch £18 per night, including 2 people. Bell tents from £60 per night, including 2 people. Additional adults £5 per night, children £3 per night (£5 for the bell tent).

caolasnacon

Kinlochleven, Argyll, PH50 4RJ 01855 831279 www.kinlochlevencaravans.com

Some Scottish campsites enjoy an epic setting shrouded by mountains; others sit by an ice-blue loch or huddle by a wee burn that ripples through the heart of the site. Caolasnacon boasts all three.

Along with its trifecta of natural assets – the mountains, the loch and the bubbling blue burn – Caolasnacon also boasts relaxed owners who let campers pitch where they want and light campfires too. Yes, they take caravans and have some statics, but they also treat campers with respect and nothing really detracts from what is definitely the most appealing campsite in the area. The pitches by the loch are ideal for kayakers and canoeists, who can just launch out into Loch Leven, while walkers will want to pitch further inland for the easiest access to the mountains – the Mamores across the water to the north, and Glen Coe's epic mountainscapes to the south.

It's a glorious scene, and you might assume that life really couldn't get any better. But it can. During one of our stays here – at that gloriously still point in the evening when shadows began lengthening as the sun slipped away – a family of otters emerged from the seaweed and undergrowth on the margins of the loch. We had to rub the disbelief from our eyes before watching them play happily in the shallows for over an hour, barely 10 metres away.

These squeak-emitting little web-toed critters aren't the only wildlife to be spotted around this scenic idyll, though. Come morning, the sky is alive with buzzards soaring across the loch, while resident golden eagles patrol the mountain slopes behind the site. The usual signs of human activity feel a safe distance away. With all this surrounding natural beauty, you could be forgiven for thinking that Caolasnacon is hundreds of miles from anywhere and therefore nearly impossible to reach, but it isn't. The main road from Glasgow to Fort William is handily just three miles away, at Glencoe.

More sedentary souls can take a trip on one of the world's great railway journeys, the West Highland Line, from the bustling nearby tourist hub of Fort William. Many new arrivals soon ditch their grand touring plans, though, and just idle by the loch soaking up the epic views and scanning the water, wild hillsides and big skies.

Caolasnacon provides a unique opportunity to get away from it all among some of the most appealing and least spoiled scenery in the land but amazingly remains within easy reach of all those modern conveniences that make camping life enjoyable, whatever the weather has in store.

WHO'S IN Tents, campervans, caravans, dogs, groups – yes.

ON SITE 50 pitches, of which those near the loch can be windy but there is some protection against the midges. Campfires allowed. Clean and efficient washrooms: not the most modern, but decent enough, with good showers, toilets, wash basins, washing-up sinks, laundry and electric hook-ups. Gas available at the farm. Undercover chemical disposal point.

OFF SITE Canoeing on Loch Leven and walking in Glen Coe are the main activities nearby – ask the owners for the best family routes around the loch and on lower terrain. For something really different, Ice Factor (01855 831100) in Kinlochleven can teach older children the basics in ice-climbing and winter skills training all year round. The Caledonian MacBrayne ferries to Gigha, Islay, Colonsay, Arran and Jura provide days out with a difference.

FOOD & DRINK The legendary Clachaig Inn (01855 811252) may infamously refuse to serve Campbells, but otherwise it's a welcoming Glen Coe pub amid epic mountain scenery. On the opposite shores of the eponymous loch, the Lochleven Seafood Café (01855 821048) in Kinlochleven is one of Europe's finest places to savour shellfish. Other choices here include The Bothan Bar (01855 831100) open from 4pm, in the Ice Factor, which is quite trendy, and MacDonald's (01855 831539), not to be confused with the fast-food joint, which offers traditional hotel fare as well as packed lunches for walks. There's also the Tail Race Inn (01855 831772), a simple pub doing simple food, and the Highland Getaway Restaurant and Balcony Bar (01855 831258).

GETTING THERE From the A82 (Glasgow–Fort William road), take the B863 (right) in Glencoe, signposted to Kinlochleven. The site is 3 miles further on the left.

PUBLIC TRANSPORT Highland Country's (01463 222244) no. 44 bus runs between Fort William and Kinlochleven and passes by the site entrance.

OPEN April–October inclusive (or Easter, if earlier).

THE DAMAGE From £12 per night for a 2-person tent and occupants, to £23 for a large tent. If you stay 6 nights you get the 7th night free.

glen nevis holidays

Glen Nevis, Fort William, Inverness-shire PH33 6SX 01397 702191 www.glen-nevis.co.uk

The children's play area may be small but that's because the surroundings are so big. Set below the 'mountain of heaven', Glen Nevis Holidays is in the middle of the UK's largest and most spectacular natural playground.

Towering at 4,408ft, Ben Nevis is a hulk of a mountain, a vast, looming chunk of rock known to many Scots simply as 'The Ben'. It's probably not the most classically proportioned of all Scotland's mountains, but it certainly catches the eye, and the wider setting is undoubtedly one of the most beautiful in the country. The feet of the mountain roll into a rugged natural landscape enlivened by the sound of water and garnished with herds of shaggy Highland cattle grazing the valley floor. The place is picture-postcard-ready. In fact, trawl the local post office and the cards simply don't do it justice – this is one you'll have to see in the flesh, and Glen Nevis Holidays is the perfect place from which to experience this sublime landscape. Nestled in the narrow plain below the mountains, it couldn't be closer to the action if it tried. This is a campsite to which the approach should definitely be savoured. The quiet, valley-floor road offers a glorious glimpse of what awaits you. Heather-clad mountains cascade down on either side and fleeting shots of the River Nevis flicker into view as it rambles along next to the road. The campsite entrance is not hard to miss, fronted by its reception and shop building and, beyond, the vast space of a 30-acre site anticipates your arrival.

Thirty acres probably sounds like a lot. And it is. This is a large site, catering to a high demand for proper out-of-doors accommodation around these parts. But don't let this put you off: the campsite has a thoroughly welcoming feel and the manicured fields are nicely screened by trees and hedges. There are nine different camping fields in total, four for motorhomes and five for those looking for a soft patch of grass to peg down on. In summer the tent fields are a wonderfully sociable place, full of outdoorsy types spreading their maps across the grass and planning the next day's hiking. Facilities are excellent and the picnic tables dotted around each field are a welcome touch.

As lovely as this site is, though, it is inevitably overshadowed by the surroundings, and you won't be sitting at those picnic tables for long. Take the low-level walk along to the dramatic Nevis gorge, with impressive falls and rapids that open into a secret valley carpeted with wildflowers. For something more challenging, tackle Ben Nevis itself or join one of the neighbouring (and quieter) routes on the next-door peaks. On a clear day you can enjoy the full, awe-inspiring vistas below, with the U-shaped glacial valley streaming off towards Loch Eil in the distance.

From here it's easy to see what makes Glen Nevis such a special place.

WHO'S IN Tents, campervans, caravans, groups (by prior arrangement), well-behaved dogs – yes.

ON SITE 5 tent fields (some with electrical hook-ups) and 4 separate caravan and campervan fields with hardstandings (all with electricity). Washrooms with toilets, showers, basins, razor points and handdryers. Private disabled facilities. Launderette and ironing facilities. Covered dish-washing and food prep area. Children's play area and games field. Well-stocked onsite shop. Guests have access to 1000 spectacular acres of the Glen Nevis Estate.

OFF SITE Walking is the main activity here, with endless routes strung out in all directions. Many will try to take on Ben Nevis – a challenge that's manageable for older children in good weather but not for the youngest. To enjoy the views without blisters you can also take a gondola (01397 705825) to the top from Fort William. Inverlochy Castle (01397 702177), the Caledonian Canal, the West Highland Museum (01397 702169) and iconic Eilean Donan Castle (01599 555202) are also nearby.

FOOD & DRINK The Glen Nevis Restaurant (01397 705459) is on the edge of the site, where they serve a buffet breakfast, lunch, coffee, cakes and snacks. Just down the road, the Ben Nevis Inn (01397 701227) is the definition of a rustic pub. Food is served from midday.

GETTING THERE Approaching Fort William from the north you'll see a campsite sign on the roundabout just after you cross the River Nevis on the way into town. Follow this and it's impossible to miss. If approaching from the south, stay on the A82 and you'll see a signpost at the second roundabout after bypassing the town.

PUBLIC TRANSPORT A daily Stagecoach bus runs from Fort William to Glen Nevis 2 or 3 times a day in summer. Regular trains run to Fort William from Glasgow and you can travel direct from London on the Caledonian Sleeper.

OPEN Mid March–early November.

THE DAMAGE Tents: adults £9, children (5–15yrs) £2, under-5s free, cars £2. Caravans/campervans: pitch £13.50, adults £3.50, children (5–15yrs) £2. Electricity £4.50. Wi-Fi £5.

ardnamurchan

Ormsaigberg, Kilchoan, Acharacle, Inverness-shire PH36 4LL 01972 510766 www.ardnamurchanstudycentre.co.uk

The view, the wildlife (otters, pine martens, sea eagles and golden eagles) and the serene and secret beaches make the journey to the Ardnamurchan Peninsula worth every moment. The journey home is the only sad part.

Ancient Celtic traditions say that over the western sea, beyond the edge of any map, lies the afterlife. Sitting at Ardnamurchan campsite it's certainly easy to believe, as you watch the sun torch the ocean between the scattered Hebrides, that you're as close as you can get to Heaven on Earth. The site clings to the coast just a few miles from the tip of a rocky finger of land, approached via a ferry and a sinuous single-track road that makes getting here an escapade in itself. Situated to the west of the beautiful village of Kilchoan, the site inhabits a small south-facing croft boasting stunning views down the Sound of Mull to Morven and Mull. This far-flung location makes it the most westerly campsite on the British mainland.

Remarkably, it has been brought into being by one man, Trevor Potts, who has turned an old croft into this Elysian camping field. The site may seem rough-and-ready at first glance, but as you settle in you'll appreciate just how much Trevor has done to make it welcoming. Every pitch has been cut from the slope and levelled by Trevor's own hand, and he has recently vanquished a field of seven-foot-high bracken to open up a new camping area. It was Trevor who single-handedly built the ablutional stuff with recycled materials, and he even constructed the replica of Shackleton's remarkable little boat that stands next to the campsite. There is nothing fancy or arty about what Trevor has done here, but he did it all himself and everything fits in neatly with the surroundings. It feels like you're camping on a genuine working highland croft – which is what this site used to be. Pitches range from neat nooks with hook-ups near the washblock to wilder spots closer to the shore. If you camp right at the bottom of the slope you will be lulled to sleep by the wash of wave on rock. If the weather is boisterous, you may even find the spray will splash your tent. The foreshore is rough, rocky and just right for a scramble. You can catch creatures in the rockpools, throw stones at the waves or simply watch the ferries weaving their way along the sound.

So, what else does the Ardnamurchan Peninsula have to tempt you? Well, some of the loveliest beaches on the planet can be found nearby, as well as a remarkable remnant of a volcano nearby. Just a few miles away are the glorious sands of Sanna, through an almost extra-terrestrial landscape of steep cliffs and snaggle-toothed ridges. Further on around the coast, in Swordle Bay, archaeologists unearthed a Viking burial boat, virtually intact, in 2011, although only a mound of stones marks the spot. Back at the site, it's not hard to understand why people have been coming here for thousands of years.

WHO'S IN Tents, campervans, groups, dogs – yes. Large motorhomes, caravans – no.

ON SITE Basic and quaintly ramshackle, with 2 loos and 2 surprisingly powerful showers (flourished with decorative flowers and a whale skeleton!), laundry and dishwashing facilities. 20 pitches and 4 campervan hook-ups. You can also hire a caravan or a bothy. Washing-up area with fridge. internet access. No campfires.

OFF SITE Stroll on the sandy beach at Sanna. Visit the lighthouse at Ardnamurchan Point and climb the tower (01972 510210). Nearby Ben Hiant is a terrific wee mountain with superb views. You can also pop over to Tobermory on Mull by ferry from Kilchoan (0800 066 5000), which makes a nice change from all the outdoor activities.

FOOD & DRINK There's a fun coffee shop in an old stable at the Ardnamurchan Lighthouse. Bar meals and finer evening dining are on offer at the Kilchoan House Hotel (01972 510200), 1½ miles away. Guests are also encouraged to bring their own musical instruments along to create impromptu music in the public bar. There's also good food available at the Sonachan Hotel (01972510211) on the way to the lighthouse.

GETTING THERE From the A82 take the ferry from Corran to Ardgour, then the A861 for 25 miles to Salen, then turn left onto the B8007. On reaching Kilchoan, follow the lane along the coast and the site is almost at the end of this.

PUBLIC TRANSPORT City Link buses (08705 505050) and trains (01397 703791) run to Fort William, from where Shiel Buses run a daily service to Kilchoan post office (01967 431272), which is less than a mile from the campsite.

OPEN April–September.

THE DAMAGE Adults £9; children (5–14yrs) £4; under-5s free. Dogs £1. Hook-ups £4.

inver coille

Invermoriston, Inverness-shire IV63 7YE 01320 351224 www.inver-coille.co.uk

This is where you need to come for a real detective's getaway. Pack the telescope, bring your snorkel and board the good ship Inver Coille. We're off to find Scotland's most famous monster.

'At the end of the woods' is the meaning of this campsite's Gaelic name, and it's a rather fitting one given the way it snuggles among trees, which are too thin to be considered a forest but not quite sparse enough to give unbroken views of Loch Ness. Stroll through the pines across the road and you quickly find your way to the waterside, though, where the 23-mile-long waters unfold before you. The loch holds more water than every lake in England and Wales put together – plus a famously murky monster that still draws tourist crowds.

A family-run site, Inver Coille comes with all the wonderful gifts that a newly created campsite offer. The tent pitches themselves are beautifully rustic and unaltered – there are no electrical hook-ups and no lines of static caravans to blight the landscape – while the facilities are all brand new, including a communal campfire with mountain views, showers, toilets and washing-up sinks with water filtered from a burn that runs through the campsite. There are also a couple of glamping options: a pre-pitched bell tent and two modern-looking geo-domes, each positioned on a flat wooden platform and furnished inside with proper beds.

The intimate atmosphere of the campsite suits the tranquil surroundings, with tents pitched on two grassy meadows enclosed by trees. A maximum

of 40 pitches ensures everyone has space. Most folks are walkers or cyclists following the routes along the loch shores. The Great Glen way is particularly popular – a 72-mile coast-to-coast route across the highlands that passes just a few hundred metres up the slope from the campsite.

Invermoriston is the nearest village, three miles away, though you're better off heading four miles south to Fort Augustus where there's a little more going on, including an excellent visitor centre, a small museum and the scenic ending of the Caledonian Canal, where a series of five locks lead down into the loch. There are also a few good pubs and tour operators who can take you out on to the waters to search for Nessie yourself.

WHO'S IN Glampers, campers, tents, families, groups, couples, dogs – yes. Caravans, campervans, motorhomes – no.

ON SITE 20 level pitches, 20 not-so-level pitches, 2 geo-domes and a bell tent. No electrical hook-ups. Drying room facilities (ask the owners for access), a covered washing-up area and a washroom with toilets, basins, high-quality showers and hairdryers. Geo-domes have their own luxury shower rooms. Games and books are available to borrow.

OFF SITE Head to Fort Augustus (4 miles) to watch boats stepping through the Caledonian Canal locks onto Loch Ness. It's quite a sight and a wonderful place to picnic. There's also a good visitor centre (01320 345156) where you can make plans for the rest of your stay. A few miles further up the shore, Urquhart Castle (01456 450551) is well worth a visit. For those who don't want to take on the lengths of the Great Glen Way (running directly past the campsite), head around the loch to Foyers, where there's a short but spectacular walk along the gorge to a waterfall.

FOOD & DRINK An onsite shop sells essentials and the local villages have larger shops around 5 minutes' drive away. For a meal out, try The Boathouse Lochside Restaurant (01320 366682), where fresh fish & chips and traditional grub is mixed with a few Mediterranean options.

GETTING THERE From the north on the A82, after Invermoriston, the campsite is 1½ miles further on. There are big signs on the A82 you cannot miss. From the south, follow the A82 through Fort Augustus and after 4 miles you will see the signs.

PUBLIC TRANSPORT There are train stations in Inverness, Fort William and Spean Bridge, and buses run to Fort Augustus or Invermoriston and will stop at the campsite if you ask.

OPEN Camping April–end September. Bell tents May–September. Geo-domes all year (except Christmas).

THE DAMAGE Adults £8, children (3–15yrs) £5, under-3s free. See website for glamping prices.

lazy duck

Nethy Bridge, Inverness-shire PH25 3ED 01479 821092 www.lazyduck.co.uk

Breathe, unwind, relax. This tiny hideaway has just four pitches and only allows small tents. Private, peaceful and laid-back, there's nowhere better on earth to introduce your kids to the pleasures of laziness.

The Lazy Duck campsite is well named. Its resident Aylesbury Ducks are so relaxed that the site owners David and Valery once had to bring in nanny ducks as the Aylesburys were too lazy to bother hatching their own eggs. The site seems to have an equally soporific effect on campers, and new arrivals soon slip into a similarly relaxed state, as doing very little becomes the main aim of the day.

To call the Lazy Duck a campsite is misleading. It's more a chilled forest clearing, blessed with a sauna, wood-fired hot tub and a bush shower, where swings and hammocks dangle from the tall trees. It just happens to have plenty of room for four very lucky tents and their (maximum of three) inhabitants. With typical unassuming attention to detail, David and Valery and their team ask you to move on every three days to another spot to save the grass. Comforts include the Campers' Shelter, where you can relax by a chimenea in the evening and meet your fellow lotus-eaters, while other welcome additions are the Woodman's Hut, a seriously romantic log cabin-style getaway for two; The Duck's Nest, an enviable retreat for couples right on the waterside; and the Lambing Bothy, which stands alone among the nuzzling Soay sheep and free-range hens.

The larch-built, wood-fired sauna is not just an afterthought, either, with a small chillout area by the sauna room where you can light a candle, burn a little essential oil and listen to the collection of ambient CDs. The views, both here and all around the site, are sublime, with the heather moorland and patches of Caledonian forest stretching out in front, while the peaks of the Cairngorms lurk to the rear.

Once you've managed to rouse yourself from this wanton relaxation, even setting out on a walk requires little effort, as the long-distance Speyside Way passes nearby. The area is also very popular with mountain bikers and you can cycle on the Speyside Way itself, around the Abernethy Forest or the Rothiemurchus Estate. The forest and estate are both highly regarded, with a variety of terrains from smooth forest roads to tough muddy single tracks. In winter there are ski slopes nearby; and 'hutters' (there's no camping from November to May) are advised to bring their toboggan if they fancy a spot of sledging.

Back at the campsite, the eponymous ducks are often joined in the ponds and Fhuarain Burn by myriad other forms of birdlife and red squirrels, roe and red deer, and the odd capercaillie can be spotted within the surrounding forest. You can also tackle the Spey in a canoe or kayak, or just sample some of its famous produce on a choice of distillery tours – this is serious whisky countrY. After a few drams, a swing in a hammock is the perfect recreation at a site where relaxation is practically mandatory. Just ask those ducks.

WHO'S IN Small families, small tents – yes. Caravans, campervans, dogs, big groups, young groups – no.

ON SITE 4 pitches for smallish tents for up to a maximum of 3 people. Campfires enouraged (in 2 chimeneas). Wet-weather cooking facilities. Sauna and wood-fired hot tub (accommodates up to 6) available for a nominal charge. Hammocks and swings. Toilet, bush shower and wash basin close by the camping area. Washing-up space, 'bush shower'. Free-range eggs when available plus veggies and bags of salad.

OFF SITE The site is within the Cairngorms National Park, which has numerous outdoor activities plus the Cairngorm Mountain Railway (01479 861261). The area is also home to the wonderful Cairngorm Reindeer Centre (01479 861228), where you can feed, stroke and walk among these friendly animals. Situated in the centre of the National Park, visitors also get excellent mountain views when they follow the herder up to the mountain enclosure. The resort town of Aviemore has plenty of wet-weather options, shops, cafés and a swimming pool.

FOOD & DRINK A fishmonger visits on Wednesdays and nearby Nethy Bridge has a hotel bar, fine dining hotel, post office and store and the superb Balliefurth Farm Shop (01479 821245). The Old Bridge Inn (01479 811137), on the edge of Aviemore, serves local Moray fish and Speyside steaks. Elsewhere, the daytime-only Druie Restaurant Café in Rothiemurchus (01479 810005) has sandwich and cake options as does the beautifully rustic café-cum-bird-hide at Inshriach Nursery (01540 651287).

GETTING THERE From Aviemore, follow the A95 towards Grantown-on-Spey. After 8 miles, turn right towards Nethy Bridge. Enter the village at Station Road and do a quick left and right to cross the B970. You'll find the campsite 1 mile ahead signposted on the edge of the village.

PUBLIC TRANSPORT Stagecoach Highlands run services to Nethy Bridge from Aviemore and Grantown-on-Spey.

OPEN Camping from May–October. Lambing Bothy, Woodman's Hut, Duck's Nest and 8-bed hostel open all year.

THE DAMAGE £15 for tent and 1 person, £20 for 2, £25 for 3.

ace hideaways

Auchnagairn, Dunphail, Forres, Moray IV36 2QL 01309 611729 www.acehideaways.co.uk

In the far-flung county of Moray a wee gem of a campsite hides, cunningly disguised as a wild-camping spot. Scratch the surface and you'll find some more comfortable camping and glamping options and an adrenalin-packed adventure centre with something for all ages.

Ace Hideaways is a remarkable place. Enigmatic in many ways, it avoids any one, single definition and in fact makes its name as a campsite – or hideaway – for every kind of escape. The setting is one of serenity and peace – clearings in the woods with off-grid glamping accommodation and basic camping pitches – yet its adrenaline-pumping, heart-thumping adventure arm lends an altogether different atmosphere when needed: one of white-water action and paint-balling fun.

The type of holiday you're after, of course, is entirely up to you. Families and campers heading north for a quiet escape are blessed with the remoteness that Morayshire affords. The elegant, mature trees of the site reach across one another to enclose you in a cocoon of quiet, while miles of footpaths, rivers and empty open space remind you what makes this part of Scotland so special. Adrenaline addicts meanwhile can weave through the campsite footpaths to the banks of the River Findhorn, don a lifejacket and hurl themselves into its depths – be that via canoe, kayak, raft or simply plunging in on one of their cliff-jumping sessions.

Facilities-wise, things are similarly eclectic. There are a few tent pitches, three large bell tents – furnished with mattresses or bean bags – and a shepherd's hut for two (fully equipped for a luxury glamping break). Each have their own clearing in the woods, while off-grid compost toilets and gas-heated showers blend seamlessly and appropriately into the woodland surroundings. There's also a communal area for cooking, with firepits, utensils and washing-up sinks, along with a huge log table and stools, crafted out of a giant tree that blew down on the banks of the river.

There's plenty to do locally. The Findhorn Valley is typified for its rich woodland and spectacular gorges, with footpaths leading directly from the campsite. You can, in fact, walk the two miles from the campsite to Logie Steading Visitor Centre, where there's ample information on the area and its wildlife. Not that you really need to go that far. Couples in the shepherd's hut can peer from its tiny windows like birdwatchers in a hide, observing the myriad creatures of the forest, while everyone else can make do creeping quietly around with a pair of binoculars to hand. You'll be surprised just how many creatures frequent the campsite – a welcome sign of just how subtle and eco-friendly the whole place is.

WHO'S IN Tents, campervans, dogs – yes. Caravans and large motorhomes – no. Large groups can book the whole site.

ON SITE 5–10 woodland camping pitches with no electric hook-ups, space for 1–2 small campervans, 3 bell tents and a shepherd's hut. Woodland showers and composting loos, plus a well-equipped camp kitchen. Campfires are permitted. Camping pitches allow for 1 tent and up to 5 guests each. Bell tents feature mattresses and bean bags but are sparsely furnished (you'll need to bring your own bedding). Well-furnished shepherd's hut for couples only. Look out for red squirrel, roe deer, pine marten and a whole range of abundant bird- and wildlife. A whole host of activities are offered on site, including white-water rafting, tubing, kayaking, canyoning, cliff-jumping, disc golf and paintball.

OFF SITE The campsite is around 2 miles from Logie Steading Visitor Centre (01309 611378), a good starting-point for the local area. It's about 12 miles to the Moray coastline with its vast sandy beaches and fishing villages.

FOOD & DRINK The reception shop stocks a few camping essentials, plus hot drinks and chocolate bars. The closest place for a good, freshly-prepared, homemade lunch is in the café at Logie Steading (01309 611733), about 2 miles away. There's also a range of artisanal shops at Logie Steading and you can stock up on estate beef or venison, Scottish salmon, cheeses, traditional oatcakes and other goodies in the farm shop. If you'd like a decent pub meal and a walk on the beach, The Kimberley Inn (01309 690492) in Findhorn is a great choice.

GETTING THERE Leave the A940 at the turning for Logie Steading Visitor Centre. Stay on the B9007 and, after 2¼ miles, the campsite is up a track on the left.

OPEN April–October. Weather-dependent though, so get in touch if you'd like to stay outside this period.

THE DAMAGE Adults from £6; children (2–17yrs) from £3.50, under-2s free. Bell tents: adults from £11.25; children from £7.50. Shepherd's hut from £55 for 2 people.

sands

Sands Caravan & Camping, Gairloch, Wester Ross IV21 2DL 01445 712152 www.sandscaravanandcamping.co.uk

Pack your wetsuit, bring the bucket and spade and prepare to get water-happy. The beautiful beachside location of this family campsite is matched only by the serene views of Skye and the Hebrides.

The shop at Sands is possibly the most remarkably stocked campsite store in the country. So much so that, as you check in, you might think the owners James and Marie have gone a wee bit over the top. But then you pitch your tent, breathe in the sea air, look out through the dune grass at the islands and mountains and realise that champagne, home-reared Highland beef and inflatable canoes are EXACTLY what you need right now.

That's the thing about Sands: it keeps surprising you. The winding road that leads north out of Gairloch seems to be heading nowhere, then a sliver of grassy land gradually unfolds into a wide and welcoming apron bordered by swooping dunes and an epic seascape. Driving in, your first impressions are of a large caravan site, but campers have their own area of rolling duneland with plenty of tent-sized pockets for you to hide away in. This starts just down a winding track from the shop, and it's worth continuing along to check out the whole site before choosing your spot. Pitches range from secluded hollows to breezy eyries, while the spots in the southern corner are ideally placed by the site's own slipway – perfect for launching kayaks and other watery adventures. There are also 12 heated Wigwams should you fancy taking it a little easier

for a few nights. These come with firepits (campfires are not allowed anywhere else) and sublime views of the sunset as standard. Wherever you are, it won't be too long before you're winding your way through the dunes and down onto the beach to paddle in the irresistibly turquoise water. And even if this is surprisingly cold, don't worry – the shop sells wetsuits, too.

The gently sloping sands of the beach entice one and all for castle-building, swimming and general larking about. Afterwards, you can perch in the grass at the top of the dunes, taking pride in your achievements and watching the sunset over the far tip of Skye. With a beach to dig up, dunes to jump down, rocks to graze knees on and woods to go heffalump-hunting in, it's ironic that the campsite also has an adventure playground – it's not like it needs one. However, it's a beauty, and you might be glad of the games room, too – after all, it has been known to rain in north-west Scotland. There's also a large indoor cooking and washing-up area, complete with several benches, and James and Marie have just finished building a small café as well. They are also planning to lay out a few mountain-bike tracks on some adjacent land. Like there isn't enough to do here already....

WHO'S IN Tents, campervans, caravans, dogs (on leads) – yes.

ON SITE The wash-blocks are rather old but they're also huge and are kept very clean. There is a large indoor kitchen and dining space, the barn café, a dishwashing area, electric hook-ups, a laundry, a games room, plus bike and canoe hire and a children's adventure playground. The shop is very well stocked and is licensed. No campfires (except for wigwam guests).

OFF SITE The beautiful path to Flowerdale Falls, a mile south of Gairloch, offers the oppotunity for an energetic family ramble. The Gairloch Heritage Museum (01445 712287) is a great local museum that will have you stepping back in time to soak up some local history.

FOOD & DRINK The Mountain Coffee Company in Gairloch (01445 712316) has a terrific selection of outdoor and adventure books, and the cakes are pretty thrilling, too. The food at The Old Inn at Flowerdale (01445 712006) is worth seeking out, and it tastes particularly delicious if you sit outside and enjoy it under the trees by the river. Tootle around the loch to The Badachro Inn (01445 741255), which snuggles by the seashore in a sheltered bay, where you can choose from 50 malt whiskies or simply enjoy a pint of the local ale by open fires and watch the boats come and go on the peaceful waters of the loch. The Melvaig Inn (01445 771212), 6 miles from the campsite at Melvaig, is a bar/restaurant with leather sofas, pool table and wonderful views out to Skye, and it serves up sandwiches and lunches, as well as cream teas and cakes during the day. In the evening you can choose from their homemade pies and locally-caught seafood dinners.

GETTING THERE Take the A832 to Gairloch; from there follow the B8021 coastal road north towards Melvaig. The Sands is 4 miles along this road on the left.

PUBLIC TRANSPORT There is a daily bus from Inverness to Gairloch. From there you will need to walk or hitch a ride.

OPEN April–September.

THE DAMAGE Tent and car plus 2 people £16–£18. Extra adults £7, children (5–16yrs) £3.

Find and book your perfect camping holiday

To instantly check availability for hundreds of camping and glamping sites and book at the best price, visit

www.coolcamping.com

Botany Camping (p78)

index

acknowledgements

Cool Camping: Kids (3rd edition)
Series Concept & Series Editor: Jonathan Knight
Editors: Martin Dunford, James Warner Smith
Editorial Assistants: Andrew Day, David Jones
Researched, Written and Photographed by:
David Bowern, Anna Chapman, Dan Davies,
Sophie Dawson, Andrew Day, Keith Didcock,
David & Jane Hart, David Jones, Scott Manson,
Andrea Oates, Sam Pow, Paul Sullivan,
Hayley Spurway, Clover Stroud, Dave Swindells,
Alexandra Tilley Loughrey, Ally Thompson,
James Warner Smith, Dixie Wills, Richard Waters,
Harriet Yeomans
Designers: Kenny Grant, Diana Jarvis
Proofreader: Leanne Bryan
Index: Helen Smith

Published by: Punk Publishing, 81 Rivington
Street, London EC2A 3AY

UK Sales: Compass IPS Limited, Great West
House, Great West Road, Brentford TW8 9DF;
020 8326 5696; sales@compass-ips.co.uk

The publishers and authors have done their
best to ensure the accuracy of all information in
Cool Camping: Kids, however, they can accept no
responsibility for any injury, loss or inconvenience
sustained by anyone as a result of information
contained in this book.

We hope you've enjoyed reading *Cool Camping:
Kids* and that it has inspired you to visit some of
the places featured. The campsites in this book
represent a small selection of the sites approved
and recommended online at coolcamping.com.
Visit the website to find more campsites and to
leave your own reviews, search availability and
book camping and glamping accommodation
across the UK and the rest of Europe.